Aspen High Country

The Geology
A Pictorial Guide to Roads & Trails

by David Laing and
Nicholas Lampiris

Available from:
Thunder River Press
Box 10935
Aspen, Colorado 81611

COVER: A place for mending spirits: looking up Hunter Creek to the Williams Mountains.

© Copyright 1980, Thunder River Press, 1980, Aspen, Colorado. All rights reserved. No part of this publication may be reproduced, stored in a retrieval system, or transmitted in any form or by any means, electronic, mechanical, photocopying, recording, or otherwise, without the prior written permission of publisher.

Printed in the United States of America
Library of Congress Catalog Card Number: 80-51131
ISBN: 0-9604274-0-6

Table of Contents

About This Guide	1
The Geologic Setting	3
The Geologic Record at Aspen	7
Road and Trail Logs: How to Use Them	31
Road Logs	33
Independence Pass Road	33
Castle Creek Road	43
Woody Creek Road	51
Lincoln Creek Road	56
Maroon Creek Road	60
Trail Logs	67
Ute Trail	67
Rio Grande Trail	78
Buckskin Pass Trail	86
Independence Lake Trail	93
Hunter Creek Trail	99
Grizzly Lake Trail	102
Road and Trail Maps	109
Glossary	115
Bibliography	130
Geologic Map of the Aspen Area	

About This Guide

With this guidebook, you can either physically travel the roads and trails of the Aspen area, or follow them in words and pictures. Either way, the objective is to lead you to a deeper understanding and appreciation of the fascinating geology of this uniquely beautiful region of the Rocky Mountains.

The plan of the book has been to select those roads and trails which best epitomize the varied aspects of Aspen's geological environment, and to cover these in detail by road and trail logs, explaining each new feature and its Earth-historical context as it is encountered along the road or trail, thus building up, by tangible steps, a picture of what is here, how it got here, and what it's doing here.

By the time you've covered all the roads and trails described in this guide, you should have a sufficient knowledge and understanding of the geological features and processes in the Aspen area to be able to identify similar features and processes in other parts of the Aspen area and in nearby regions of the Rocky Mountains.

So, if you wonder why your favorite trail may have been omitted, this is the reason. A comprehensive coverage of all roads and trails would be redundant, and it would leave little to fuel the fire of discovery, which we hope to ignite with this book.

No previous knowledge of geology is assumed. The next chapter discourses on the geologic history of the Aspen area. You may wish to read this for background before setting forth with the logs. You may find the glossary in the back helpful.

The five road logs precede the six trail logs. The order in which they are arranged seems a logical one to us for the objective of a stepwise introduction to the total geological picture, but each log is quite independent of the others, and little should be lost or gained by taking them in a different order.

While we have taken pains to ensure that all our interpretations are correct, there remains the possibility of error. Anticipating a second edition, we would be very grateful for any corrections or comments that may come to mind. These should be addressed to us at Post Office Box 10935, Aspen, Colorado 81611.

We are indebted to several individuals for their valuable assistance, advice, and encouragement in various aspects of the book. Among these are Tom L. Heidrick, Jennifer S. Laing, Robert Scarborough, and Joseph P. Wise. We, however, take sole responsibility for all statements of fact and interpretations that follow.

Special thanks go to J. Gill Wright, whose encouragement and support made it all possible.

The Geologic Setting

Few places have a geologic record that is richer than Aspen's. Not only is this record a long one, spanning about two billion years from the Upper Precambrian Era to the present, but it's also replete with events, all of which have contributed to the fabric of the Rocky Mountain environment that we so enjoy and appreciate today.

The fundamental frame of reference for the discussion of Aspen geology that follows is the geologic map inside the back cover of the book. This map shows the various rock units, or formations, that are exposed at the land surface within a 25- by 30-mile rectangle centered on Aspen.

Rocks are formed in various ways, and they have different ages. In Aspen, there are *sedimentary rocks,* including (a) chemical precipitates like limestone, dolomite and gypsum, that have been deposited from seawater, and (b) *clastic,* or fragmental rocks, including shale, siltstone, sandstone, and conglomerate, that have been formed by the slow chemical and mechanical breakdown of pre-existing rocks, followed by their transportation—and ultimately deposition—by running water, flowing ice, or wind, as mud, silt, sand, and gravel.

There are also *igneous rocks,* like granite and basalt, which were formed by the melting of other rocks deep within the Earth's crust or upper mantle. *Metamorphic rocks,* like gneiss, were formed where igneous rocks invaded sedimentary rocks and lavas, and changed their appearance and mineral contents by supplying a great deal of heat and pressure.

These different rock types are shown on the geologic map by certain standard patterns which are explained in the accompanying key.

Some of Aspen's rock units were formed over a billion years ago, and some are being formed today. On the geologic map, rock formation ages are shown in a general way by color, as is apparent in the key.

In the concise geologic history of the Aspen area that follows, we attempt to relate the various rock units to the geologic events that were responsible for their formation. It's important to understand that these events are not independent in time and space. It isn't enough simply to state that "a great mountain uplift occurred about 290 million years ago in central Colorado." Events such as this one are invariably tied in with the much larger framework of sea-floor spreading and continental drift. The acceptance and development of this unifying theory of geology since the late 1960's has made it possible to understand why such events happened when and where they did.

Happily, the concepts of sea-floor spreading are so simple that they are often taught in grade school science classes. The Earth's crust is broken by a coarse network of cracks which outlines seven major crustal plates. The cracks are mainly of two kinds: *spreading* and *subducting.* In a spreading crack, or rift, basalt lava wells up from the Earth's mantle to fill the rift as it spreads. In a subducting crack, or subduction zone, the advancing edge of one crustal plate is being drawn under beneath the adjacent edge of another plate. Lavas erupted above subduction zones are of a distinctive type known as *andesite* after the Andes mountains, which are located above a major subduction zone on the western edge of the South American plate.

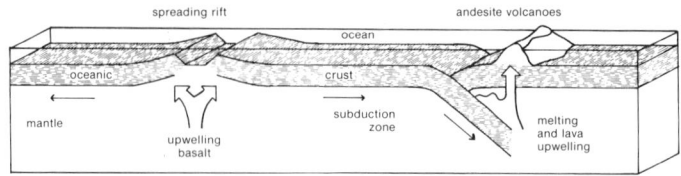

Andesite is intermediate in composition between basalt—the rock material of the oceanic plates—and granite, the most characteristic rock material of the continents. Granite is lighter than basalt, and therefore the continents float on top of the denser basaltic plates. This explains why the continents invariably have higher elevations than the ocean basins.

Normally, continents can't be subducted (northern India, plunging beneath southern Asia, is an exception, which produced the truly exceptional Himalayas). If a subducting basaltic plate carries an overlying granitic continent to its subduction zone at another plate margin, the continental margin will normally stop at the subduction zone (as in A, B, and C, below). What happens then

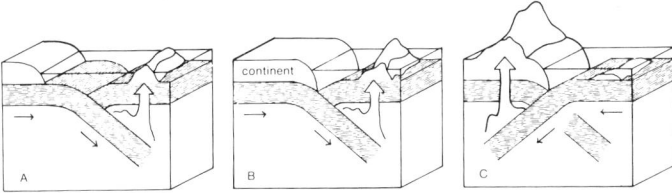

depends on whether the other, opposing plate is basaltic (oceanic) or granitic (continental). If it's granitic (as in X and Y, below), the two continental plates will normally weld together at their edges, thereby forming a supercontinent. If the other plate is basaltic (as in A, B, and C, above), the subduction zone will simply reverse direction, and the opposing plate will begin to be subducted beneath the continental margin.

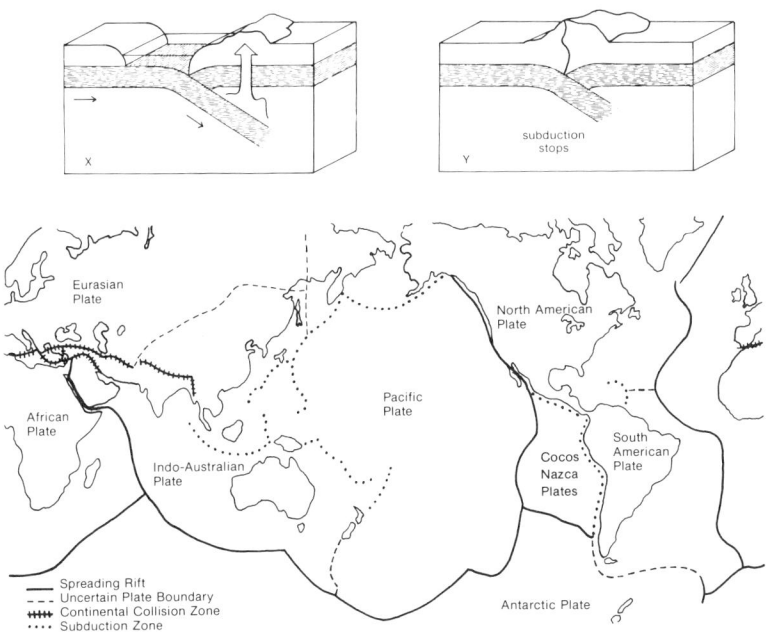

On the world map, above, notice that there is no continent overlying the Pacific plate, while the western half of the

North American plate is overlain by the continent of North America. The North American plate is drifting westward from the Mid-Altantic Ridge. The Pacific plate is drifting northwestward, forming a shear zone, or *transform fault*, along the west coast of North America, of which the San Andreas fault is a manifestation. On the east edge of the Pacific plate is a spreading rift, the East Pacific Rise. Between this and the west coast of South America is the northeastward-drifting Cocos plate, which is being subducted beneath the western edge of the North American plate.

This is only the latest configuration in a perpetually changing pattern of plate interactions. All the geological features in the Aspen area, and anywhere else on the globe, must ultimately be referred to the dynamic framework of *plate tectonics*. The continental plates are subjected to compressive, tensional and shearing stresses (squeezing, pulling and slipping) as the underlying basaltic plates interact with each other's variable rates and directions of motion.

With this very brief introduction to modern geological theory out of the way, we proceed now to the detailed chronology of the events that built Aspen's geological environment as we see and enjoy it today.

The Geologic Record at Aspen

      This is a rather detailed chronology of the geologic events and their associated rock units in the Aspen area. We have subdivided the roughly two billion year record into seven very unequal time intervals, each characterized by a distinctive geological environment, or style, that dominated the interval.

      The intervals are subdivided by significant geologic EVENTS, and the corresponding ROCK UNITS. The geologic periods below the dates in the left hand column, preceded by Early, Middle, or Upper, correspond to the geologic symbols as they appear on the geologic map inside the back cover. The units are numbered in chronological order for easy reference from the road and trail logs.

Million Years Ago	Geologic Events and Rock Units
1900-570 Upper Precambrian	**ANCIENT MOUNTAIN SYSTEMS**
1900-1700 Late Precambrian	EVENT: A great thickness of mud, volcanic debris and coarse, submarine mudflow deposits (1) was laid down in an offshore marine basin in the Aspen area. The basin probably lay over a subduction zone, but plate tectonic relationships are largely unknown.

1900-1700 Upper Precambrian	ROCK UNIT 1: *Biotite gneiss.* Black and white banded, crystalline; metamorphosed from marine basin deposits. Best seen east of Weller Campground on north side of Highway 82. Maximum thickness unknown.
1700 Late Precambrian	EVENTS: The marine basin deposits were uplifted, deformed, and intruded by granodiorite (2) probably during an episode of rapid subduction (drawing under) of the basaltic ocean floor beneath the western continental margin. Deformation was accompanied, and followed, by mountain-building.
1700 Upper Precambrian	ROCK UNIT 2: *Granodiorite.* Gray, unbanded, coarsely crystalline. May be derived, at least in part, from melting of marine basin deposits in a subduction zone. Best seen along Highway 82 on east side of Independence Pass.
1470-1250 Late Precambrian	EVENTS: Widespread intrusion of quartz monzonite (3), a granitic rock, took place in the Aspen area. Further mountain building and metamorphism occurred, probably associated with renewed rapid subduction of an oceanic plate.
1470 Upper Precambrian	ROCK UNIT 3: *Quartz monzonite.* Gray, unbanded, coarsely crystalline. May be partly derived from melting of oceanic basin deposits. Best seen at the Grottoes, one mile east of Weller Campground on the east side of Highway 82.
1400-570 Late Precambrian	EVENTS: The Earth's crust was broadly uplifted, but it remained stable for a long time, during which stream erosion reduced the ancient mountains until a widespread erosional surface of low relief was formed. The products of erosion were spread out in rather thick deposits of sand and mud to the south, west, and north of Colorado.
850 Late Precambrian	EVENTS: North America probably began to split away from another continent to the west, causing high angle faulting at Grand Canyon and the eruption of oceanic basalt within the thick sedimentary deposits of the continental margin in Nevada.

570-313 Cambrian to Mississippian	**SHALLOW MARINE INVASIONS**
540-470 Late Cambrian to Early Ordovician	EVENTS: Subduction zones formed on both the east and west coasts. In the latter, basaltic Pacific Ocean floor began to be conveyed eastward under the lighter, granitic continental margin. Andesite lavas were erupted in Nevada. Northwest of the Transcontinental Arch (a highland between Arizona and South Dakota) the continental surface sank sufficiently to permit a shallow, eastward invasion by the Pacific Ocean. Beach sand (4) was laid down by the advancing shoreline, while limestone (5) was deposited in clear, warm water west of the shore. As the shoreline migrated eastward, limestone was deposited on top of beach sand.
510 Upper Cambrian	ROCK UNIT 4: *Sawatch Quartzite,* mapped with 5-8. White quartz sandstone, strongly cemented with silica. Originally beach sand. Maximum thickness 250 feet. Best seen as white, angular chunks on the Ute Trail.
505 Upper Cambrian	ROCK UNIT 5: *Peerless Formation,* mapped with 4&6-8. Orange-gray to brown dolomitic sandstone, sandy dolomite and minor shale. Transitional between 4 and 6. Maximum thickness 150 feet. Poorly exposed due to low resistance to erosion. Usually covered with soil or landslide debris.
500 Lower Ordovician	ROCK UNIT 6: *Manitou Dolomite*, mapped with 4, 5, 7, & 8. Gray dolomite with irregular, parallel bands of gray chert. The dolomite weathers buff, the chert white. Originally limy mud from chemical precipitation of carbonates from seawater. Maximum thickness 250 feet. Best exposed at the top of the Ute Trail in steeply up-tilted outcrops.
470 Early Ordovician	EVENTS: Rapid ocean floor subduction began along both the eastern and western continental margins, creating strong compression, which raised the continental surface, causing the shallow sea to drain away from the land. On the eastern seaboard,

the Taconic Mountains were uplifted.

445
Middle
Ordovician

EVENTS: Reduced resistance between the overriding western continental margin and the underthrusting Pacific Ocean floor initiated a second cycle of continental subsidence northwest of the Transcontinental Arch, accompanied by marine invasion and the deposition of sand and lime.

395-370
Early
Devonian

EVENTS: This second marine cycle was closed by increasing compression of the continent caused by subduction on its margins. This again raised the land surface, causing the sea to recede. Subsequent erosion removed all upper Ordovician and Silurian rocks from the Aspen area.

353
Late
Devonian

EVENTS: The proto-Atlantic Ocean closed, bringing northwest Africa up against the eastern seaboard of North America. This created an unyielding force opposing the underthrusting of the Pacific Ocean floor beneath the west coast. The powerful east-west compression resulted in widespread warping and buckling of the continental crust, mainly on its thinner, softer margins. A broad belt of deformation extended from Labrador to Georgia (the Acadian Mountains), then west into Texas and Oklahoma. Another extended north-south through Nevada (the Antler Mountains).

In the Rocky Mountain region, another shallow marine invasion occurred, but simultaneously several broad uplifts began to rise (the Ancestral Rocky Mountains). In Colorado, two linear uplifts developed: the Ancestral Front Range rose along a north-northwesterly trend across the center of the state, and the Ancestral Uncompahgre Range rose along a northwesterly trend across the southwest quadrant of the state. Between these two uplifts, a broad valley, the Central Colorado Trough, developed. The existence of the uplifts at this time is inferred from the thinning of contemporary sedimentary deposits over the sites of the ranges (especially the Ancestral Front Range) and from the presence of shale at the base of the Chaffee Formation (7), derived from the erosion of the Ancestral Front

Range.

The Chaffee shale is only a small part of a vast blanket of putrid, black mud that was laid down in the shallow, stagnant inland sea that covered most of the rising continent at that time. Farther east, an equivalent black mud is known as the Chattanooga Shale.

360-345 Upper Devonian	ROCK UNIT 7: *Chaffee Formation,* mapped with 4-6 & 8. Lower part *(Parting Member)* light tan sandstone and varicolored shale. Originally sands and muds of a river delta fed from highlands to the east. Maximum thickness 100 feet. Upper part *(Dyer Dolomite Member)* gray dolomite. Originally lime mud deposited in a warm, shallow sea. Maximum thickness 100 feet. Best seen near the base of the west wall of Spar Gulch on Aspen Mountain.
345 Early Mississippian	EVENTS: The land was regionally uplifted, and the sea retreated due to increased compression of the continent between Africa and the underthrusting Pacific Ocean floor.
342-338 Early Mississippian	EVENTS: The land surface settled again, and another shallow marine invasion occurred due to release of compression, perhaps as a result of slower subduction on the west coast. Beach sand and lime (8) were deposited in the Central Colorado Trough.
342-338 Lower Mississippian	ROCK UNIT 8: *Leadville Limestone,* mapped with 4-7. Lower part (*Gilman Sandstone Member*) dolomitic sandstone and breccia. Originally beach sand from the shores of the Ancestral Front Range uplift. Upper part thin-bedded dolomite grading upward into massive limestone. Maximum thickness (both members) 200 feet. Best seen on the upper west slope of Spar Gulch on Aspen Mountain.
338 Early Mississippian / Late Mississippian	EVENTS: Regional uplift of the land began again due to renewed compression. Erosion removed the top of the Leadville Limestone.

313 Late Mississippian/ Early Pennsylvanian	EVENT: Regional uplift continued at an increasing rate.
313-151 Pennsylvanian/ Upper Jurassic	**THE ANCESTRAL ROCKIES**
313-300 Early Pennsylvanian	EVENTS: The Ancestral Front Range rose from the sea west of the site of Denver (it had also been emergent about 50 million years previously, as mentioned above) marking the beginning of a long period of intensifying east-west compression of the continent. Again, putrid mud (9) was deposited in the Central Colorado Trough.
313-300 Lower Pennsylvanian	ROCK UNIT 9: *Belden Formation*. Dark limestone and dolomite, and black oil shale with minor sandstone lenses. Originally swampy mud from streams flowing into the Central Colorado Trough from the rising Ancestral Front Range. Maximum thickness obscured by faulting and flowage, but probably about 800 feet. Poorly exposed. Best seen in mine dumps on Smuggler Mountain.
300-293 Middle Pennsylvanian	EVENTS: A major uplift of the Ancestral Uncompahgre Range occurred. Mud and sand eroded from its flanks (10) was deposited in the Central Colorado Trough. Northwest of Aspen, salts (11) precipitated out from evaporating seawater in a basin with restricted circulation.
300-293 Middle Pennsylvanian	ROCK UNIT 10: *Minturn Formation*. Tan sandstone, shale and limestone. Originally flood plain sand and mud washed north-eastward by rivers flowing off the rapidly rising Ancestral Uncompahgre Range into the Central Colorado Trough. Maximum thickness 3000 feet. Best seen along the Castle Creek Road about six miles south of Aspen. Also known as the *Gothic Formation*.

300-293 Middle Pennsylvanian	ROCK UNIT 11: *Eagle Valley Formation.* Gray to red shale, sandstone, and limestone with increasing amounts of gypsum and halite toward the northwest. Originally floodplain/tidal flat mud and sand washed from the rising Ancestral Front and Uncompahgre Ranges, and salt deposits where the circulation of seawater through the Central Colorado Trough was restricted by rapid sediment accumulation and the building of algal reefs. Maximum thickness about 2500 feet. Best seen along Woody Creek about a mile west of Lenado.
293-270 Late Pennsylvanian/ Early Permian	EVENTS: Both the Ancestral Front and Uncompahgre Ranges were uplifted to elevations of about 10,000 feet above sea level. Colorado, which was near the Equator at that time, was subject to tropical hurricanes. These storms produced violent floods that swept great volumes of weathered rock debris off the mountains to collect in thick deposits of gravel and mud (12) in the Central Colorado Trough, and to the east and west of the ranges. Sediment accumulation was thickest on the site of Aspen, near the center of the Trough. The contemporary climate was hot, and probably semiarid, but a good diversity of land plants was present, including seven genera of giant horsetails (Calamitales), eight genera of ferns and seed ferns, eight of giant club mosses (Lepidodendrales), three of a primitive, conifer-like order (Cordaitales), one true conifer, and six genera represented only by seeds and spore-producing structures.
293-270 Upper Pennsylvanian/ Lower Permian	ROCK UNIT 12: *Maroon Formation.* Red, limy sandstone, shale, conglomerate, and limestone with crossbedding, mud cracks, and current ripple marks. Originally mudflow deposits that spread into the Central Colorado Trough during heavy storms as the Ancestral Rocky Mountains were undergoing their period of most rapid uplift. Maximum thickness about 17,500 feet (3.3 miles!). Best seen along Maroon Creek Road and on Red Mountain.

280-230 Early Permian/ Middle Permian	EVENTS: As Africa pressed unremittingly against the eastern seaboard, broad, regional uplift of the continent occurred. The sea retreated, and dune sand was laid down in areas marginal to the Ancestral Rockies.
260-225 Middle Permian/ Late Permian	EVENTS: Intense compression and mountain building took place, on the east coast, raising the Appalachian Mountains. Eastern North America was broadly uplifted, establishing a westward drainage. Mud (13) was deposited on floodplains and tidal flats in the Rocky Mountain region. By this time, the Ancestral Rockies had been much reduced by erosion. Large reptiles and amphibians thrived in the widespread floodplain environment, but the progressive uplift of the land produced a drying trend in the regional climate. This change led to the extinction of many of the more primitive plant orders, such as the seed ferns, giant club mosses, giant horsetails, and primitive conifers, and cleared the way for the dominance of the true conifers during the following 150 million years.
243-215 Upper Permian/ Lower Triassic	ROCK UNIT 13: *State Bridge Formation,* mapped with 14. Red to tan shale, sandstone, and conglomerate with pebbles from diverse source areas; crossbedding and ripplemarks common. Originally floodplain/tidal-flat sand and mud derived from both distant eastern and local sources. Maximum thickness about 2400 feet. Best seen from the Cemetery Lane bridge over the Roaring Fork River at the west end of Aspen where the State Bridge Formation (here overturned in the Castle Creek fault zone) forms the northeastern slopes of Red Butte.
205-195 Late Triassic/ Early Jurassic	EVENTS: A spreading rift began to develop beneath the suture between North America and Africa. This heralded the beginning of the breakup of the supercontinent Pangaea, and the commencement of the slow westward drift of North America as the Atlantic Ocean basin began to open. Uplift, metamorphism, and volcanism began in the thick, sedimentary continental margin deposits of

the *Cordilleran geosyncline* from southern Arizona to Alaska, as a result of the compressional forces of westward drift over the Pacific Ocean floor. Mud and volcanic ash (14) were deposited around a low, broad uplift in central Colorado.

The environment of this time was rather uniform over a wide area that included Colorado, New Jersey, and Germany. In Petrified Forest National Park, Arizona, logs of two large conifers, *Araucarioxylon* (arrow-carry-o-ZI-lon) and *Woodworthia* have been preserved along with several other plant genera. Silica from volcanic ash, abundant in the mud deposits, replaced the cellulose in the buried logs, thereby preserving the form, but not the substance, of these ancient trees. Palm-like cycadeoids (SI-caddy-oids) and huge ferns were also present in these forests, which were inhabited by various types of large reptiles, of which the commonest was the crocodile-like phytosaur.

205-200 Upper Triassic	ROCK UNIT 14: *Chinle Formation,* usually mapped with 13. Red, limy shale, limestone, and conglomerate. Originally mud deposited on a flat coastal plain by streams flowing from nearby uplifts, and volcanic ash blown in from the southwest. Maximum thickness about 1000 feet. Best seen on the north face of Red Butte along the Rio Grande Trail (here overturned.)
200-172 Late Triassic/ Early Jurassic	EVENTS: Continued uplift and volcanism occurred in the Cordilleran geosyncline to the west. A series of four cycles of marine invasion and retreat from northwestern Canada began. Each of these extended farther than the last into the Rocky Mountain region. Collectively, these marine cycles are known as the Sundance Sea.
162-158 Late Jurassic	EVENTS: The fourth, and most extensive invasion of the Sundance Sea arrived from the north. Beach and dune sand (15) were deposited around the periphery of the sea.
162-158 Upper Jurassic	ROCK UNIT 15: *Entrada Sandstone,* mapped with 16-18. Yellowish sandstone with crossbedding and ripplemarks. Originally coastal dune sand

151-172
Upper
Jurassic/
Upper
Cretaceous

that advanced from the north with the Sundance Sea. Maximum thickness about 150 feet. Best seen from the Rio Grande Trail in a pinnacle to the north of Red Butte (here overturned).

THE CORDILLERAN PIEDMONT

151-140
Late
Jurassic

EVENTS: The Sundance Sea retreated as the *Nevadan orogeny* began in the Cordilleran geosyncline on the continental margin from Mexico to Alaska. The westward drift of the North American plate over the eastward moving Kula plate on the Pacific Ocean floor was responsible for the orogeny, which shortened the continental crust in Utah and Nevada about 40-60 miles by compressional folding and faulting between about 150 and 80 million years ago. The low-lying Cordilleran Piedmont, east of the newly risen range as far as central Nebraska, was buried beneath a blanket of sand, mud, lime and volcanic ash (16) derived from the initial uplift of the Cordillera.

Conifers (at least 6 genera) predominated in the forested areas of this vast floodplain, associated with primitive cycads (Cycadeoids) and ferns. Enormous, herbivorous dinosaurs, mostly with long necks and tails, heavy bodies, and massive limbs, roamed through the coastal swamps. Somewhat less enormous bipedal, carnivorous dinosaurs preyed upon the herbivores. These and other reptiles and amphibians, as well as a few very primitive mammals, have been excellently preserved in the Morrison Formation (16), one of the real treasure troves of the paleontological world.

151-140
Upper
Jurassic

ROCK UNIT 16: *Morrison Formation*, mapped with 15-18. Varicolored red to greenish shale, limestone, and sandstone. Originally mud, sand, and volcanic ash carried eastward by streams and wind from mountain uplifts in Nevada. Maximum thickness 530 feet. Best seen on the north face of

	Red Butte along the Rio Grande Trail (here overturned).
136-103 Early Cretaceous	EVENTS: In western Utah, the Sevier Mountains arose in a continuation, farther east, of the same compressional forces that produced the Nevadan orogeny. Erosional debris (17) from the Sevier orogeny was washed eastward into Colorado. By this time, flowering plants had begun to appear amid the dominant conifers, primitive cycads, and ferns. One of these early flowering trees bears the formidable name *Paraphyllanthoxylon utahense* (pa-ra-fill-anth-o-ZI-lon you-tah-ENT-see).
108 Lower Cretaceous	ROCK UNIT 17: *Burro Canyon Formation,* mapped with 18. White sandstone and conglomerate and greenish shale. Originally sand and mud washed eastward by streams from mountain uplifts in Utah (a nearer source than for the Morrison Formation is indicated by coarser-grained sediments). Maximum thickness about 225 feet. Poorly exposed in the Aspen area.
103-70 Early Cretaceous/ Late Cretaceous	EVENTS: Development of the *Cretaceous seaway* began as the Rocky Mountain region became warped down into a broad marine trough extending from Alaska to the Gulf of Mexico. Beach sand (18) was deposited at the seaway's advancing shoreline, while river mud (19) accumulated in deeper water offshore. The contemporary environment was similar to that of the present southeastern seaboard: warm and humid with coastal swamps, sandy beaches, border bars, lagoons, and estuaries. A variety of dinosaurs inhabited the swamplands. The Cretaceous vegetation consisted of pine with an admixture of ferns and flowering plants, including magnolia, gum, maple, walnut, fig, poplar, sycamore, palmetto, oak, cinnamon, pistachio, ash, lotus, and willow.
103-100 Lower Cretaceous	ROCK UNIT 18: *Dakota Sandstone,* mapped with with 15-17. Light brown sandstone and minor gray, carbonaceous shale. Originally beach and

	lagoon sand. Maximum thickness about 200 feet. Best seen on the north side of the Rio Grande Trail just west of Red Butte where a railroad cut passes through the formation.
100-75 Upper Cretaceous	ROCK UNIT 19: *Mancos Shale*. Dark gray shale with a limestone bed (the Fort Hays Member) in the lower part. Originally mud washed eastward from rising mountains in Utah. The limestone bed records the maximum extent of the Cretaceous seaway, 88 million years ago. Maximum thickness about 5200 feet. Best seen on the Rio Grande Trail west of Red Butte.
81 Late Cretaceous	EVENTS: The westward drift direction of the North American plate shifted southward abruptly by about 30 degrees, coincident with nearly a doubling of the rate of movement. This placed a strong, shearing stress on the continent, which would soon be expressed in the rising of a third generation of mountain ranges in the Rocky Mountain region. The highly complex pattern of faults in the Aspen area (see the geologic map) clearly reflects this wrenching or shearing force, which tended to drag the country to the east southward with respect to the country to the west. The mountain-building episode that resulted from these shearing forces has been called the *Laramide orogeny*.
75-68 Late Cretaceous	EVENTS: Broad, regional uplift and continued heavy sedimentation in the Cretaceous seaway forced the retreat of marine waters from the Rocky Mountain region. Beach sand (20) was deposited at the receding shoreline.
75-68 Upper Cretaceous	ROCK UNIT 20: *Mesaverde Formation*. Sandstone, minor shale, and coal. Originally beach and lagoon sand from a retreating shoreline. Maximum thickness about 5100 feet. Present along the Grand Hogback southwest of Glenwood Springs, but almost entirely eroded from the Aspen area, except for a small remnant about a mile southwest of the town of Woody Creek.

72-0 Upper Cretaceous/ Quaternary	**THE LARAMIDE ROCKIES**
72-67 Late Cretaceous	EVENTS: Beneath Colorado, trending in a northeast-southwest direction from the San Juan Mountains to Boulder, a large body of igneous rock—a batholith—was formed, probably as a result of local melting of crustal rocks by the regional shearing referred to above. In places, offshoots from this batholith penetrated upward into the sedimentary rocks overlying the ancient basement. Associated with these intrusive porphyries (21) were solutions of metal sulfides in superheated water, which formed most of the rich base and precious metal deposits—lead, zinc, copper, gold, and silver—of the Colorado Mineral Belt.
72-67 Upper Cretaceous	ROCK UNIT 21: *Laramide intrusives.* Porphyries, probably derived from an underlying batholith. Poorly exposed on the ski slopes of Aspen Mountain and elsewhere.
70-65 Late Cretaceous	EVENTS: First, the Sawatch Range, east of Aspen, and then the Front Range, west of Denver, were uplifted, along with the Park and Medicine Bow Ranges (west of the Front Range and north of the Sawatch) and the Needle and Uncompahgre Ranges in southwestern Colorado (later largely buried by andesitic lavas of the San Juan volcanic field). Other mountain uplifts in Colorado at this time were the Wet (central), the San Luis (south central), and Douglas Creek (northwest). In northeastern Utah, the Uinta Range was uplifted. In many places, the outlines of these uplifts clearly show the kinds of deformity that one would expect from a shearing stress tending to pull the western part of the continent northward with respect to the eastern part. On the steep western flank of the Sawatch uplift, the pull of gravity was so intense on the five-mile-thick blanket of sedimentary rock overlying the ancient gneiss and granite basement that all the

sediments above the Belden Formation (9) broke loose and slid westward along the Elk Range thrust fault. This enormous landslide block, measuring ten to twenty miles in east-west width and probably at least fifty miles in length, slid readily along the soft, weak shales of the Belden Formation. As the block began to slide, its western edge bent upward into a large anticline, which folded over westward and eventually broke along its crest as the pressure became too great, allowing the slide block to ride westward until it finally came to rest. The Schofield syncline (extreme southwestern corner of the geologic map) is a prominent downfold that formed immediately west of the faulted anticline. The eastern part of the Elk Range, including the 14,000-foot Maroon Bells and Pyramid Peak, have been carved by stream and glacial erosion from this phenomenal landslide block, which is properly known as a *gravity glide sheet*.

65-57 Early Tertiary	EVENTS: The long, narrow Sangre de Cristo Range rose in south-central Colorado and northern New Mexico, and the Laramie Range was uplifted in southeastern Wyoming. This range gave its name to the Laramide orogeny.
53 Early Tertiary	EVENTS: The North American plate returned to approximately the same direction and rate of westward drift as it had prior to 81 million years ago. This essentially ended the Laramide orogeny, except as noted below.
53-36 Early Tertiary	EVENTS: The release of the shearing stress on the continent introduced a long interval of crustal stability. During this time, stream erosion considerably reduced the rugged, mountainous topography that had been created by the Laramide orogeny. The result was a widespread, gently rolling plain that has been called the *Rocky Mountain erosion surface*. This surface is now preserved, under a thin cover of younger sediment, on the Great Plains, and on high-level terrace remnants in the Rocky Mountains, to be discussed below. Evidently, this old erosion plain once extended from Utah to the Mis-

sissippi, broken only by the eroded remnants of the Laramide Rockies, which rose not more than 2000 feet above it.

Throughout the Laramide orogeny, and the erosional interval that followed it, the base elevation of the land was never very far above sea level, and a humid, subtropical environment prevailed, similar to that of modern Florida.

50-45
Early
Tertiary

EVENTS: The last dying effort of the Laramide orogeny produced a gentle, arcuate uplift extending from the Uinta Mountains in northeastern Utah south-eastward into the White River Plateau in northwestern Colorado to the west flank of the Elk Range southwest of Aspen. One of the most dramatic features resulting from this final Laramide pulse is the Grand Hogback monocline, which passes southeastward through Glenwood Springs along the western edge of the Elk Range gravity glide sheet. Along this linear structure, the country to the east has been raised several thousand feet relative to the country to the west, and the sedimentary strata have been turned up sharply along the hogback, as you can see as you drive into Glenwood Springs from the west. Much of this uplift, however, is due to more recent activity, as will be mentioned further on.

40-8
Middle
Tertiary/
Upper
Tertiary

POST-LARAMIDE UPLIFT AND VOLCANISM

40-20
Middle
Tertiary

EVENTS: The western seaboard of North America, in its westward drift, approached ever closer to the East Pacific Rise, a sea floor spreading rift separating two oppositely moving ocean floor plates. As it did so, the continent experienced increasing resistance against the underlying, eastward moving Farallon plate.

During this interval, igneous magma of an intermediate composition, between continental granite and oceanic basalt, welled up into the crust of the Rocky Mountain region to form intrusive bodies

(22) of various sizes, and extrusive volcanics (23 and 24). At the same time, the western United States was broadly uplifted so that the average elevation of the land was about 3000 feet above sea level. Upon the Rocky Mountain erosion surface, great volumes of andesitic lavas (23) and explosive ash-flow tuffs (24) poured out from numerous volcanic vents, often with a violence that can scarcely be imagined, since nothing in our experience, including the hydrogen bomb, could even begin to compare with the energy released by these enormous eruptions, some of which issued from vents more than ten miles across. The Grizzly caldera in the Sawatch Mountains southeast of Aspen (see the geologic map) is about nine miles in diameter. Southwest of Aspen, the White Rock Granodiorite (22) was intruded, largely along the plane of the Elk Range thrust fault. Igneous rocks from both these localities date between 34 and 29 million years ago.

These changes in the physical environment were discouraging to the diverse flora and fauna of Laramide time. With the regional uplift, the climate became cooler and drier, similar to that of northeastern Mexico today. Many plant and animal species became extinct, or were otherwise eliminated from the region, while the hardier species, like Ponderosa Pine, began to assume more dominant roles in the ecology. Of 122 plant genera known to have been present in the Laramide flora, only 27, or 22%, survived the volcanic holocaust. Of these 27, fifteen are still present in the modern Rocky Mountain flora. They are:

Alder	Goosefoot	Poplar
Bur reed	Hackberry	Spruce
Cherry	Horsetail	Sumac
Fern	Oak	Walnut
Fir	Pine	Willow

From this list, it's easy to see that by about 35 million years ago, the Rocky Mountain flora was well on its way to developing its modern aspect.

34-29 Middle Tertiary	ROCK UNIT 22: *White Rock Granodiorite.* Gray granodiorite, most probably generated by the subduction of the Pacific Ocean floor beneath the western continental margin. Best seen on the lower portions of the Grizzly Lake Trail and on the lower east slopes of Cathedral Peak south of Aspen.
34-29 Middle Tertiary	ROCK UNIT 23: *Grizzly Andesite.* Gray lava related to the White Rock Granodiorite. Best seen on the upper portions of the Grizzly Lake Trail.
34-29 Middle Tertiary	ROCK UNIT 24: *Grizzly Ash-flow Tuff.* Welded volcanic ash and glass. Originally explosive clouds of volcanic magma related to the White Rock Granodiorite. Best seen on Independence Mountain, sixteen miles east of Aspen.
35-0 Late Tertiary	EVENTS: Sections of the East Pacific Rise became progressively subducted beneath the western continental margin. As this happened, the plate tectonic relationship changed from one in which the continent was drifting westward over an eastward-moving oceanic plate to one in which the continental margin crossed the spreading rift and overlapped onto a *northwestward-moving* oceanic plate. Forces on the North American continent, therefore, changed from east-west compression to east-west tension with a shearing component tending to drag the west coast northwestward with the overlapped Pacific plate. Furthermore, upwelling of basaltic magma presumably was still going on in the subducted spreading rift beneath the continental margin.
24 Late Tertiary	EVENTS: A widespread regional uplift of several thousand feet occurred at this time. This may well have been a result of upwelling in the subducted East Pacific Rise.
24-20 Late Tertiary	EVENTS: Deep faulting of the crust due to increasing east-west tension allowed basaltic magma (25) to rise from the Earth's mantle to be erupted as lava northwest of Aspen, and in other places in the west, particularly around the periphery of the Colorado Plateau.

23-8 Upper Tertiary	ROCK UNIT 25: *Steamboat Basin Basalt* (not present in mapped area). Black, fine-grained lava. Derived from the Earth's lower crust or mantle during deep, tensional faulting of the crust. Best seen capping mesas to the northeast of Highway 82 between Glenwood Springs and Basalt.
20-11 Late Tertiary	EVENTS: While little geologic activity took place in the Aspen area during the first 6 million years of this interval, the great Cordilleran mountain range that had dominated western North America for the past 150 million years broke up under the growing crustal tension, and sank into the vast desert of the Great Basin in Nevada, western Utah, and southern Arizona. The massive mountains were fragmented into long, thin blocks between the steep, north-trending faults as the continental crust was extended in an east-west direction by some 30 to 60 miles.
14-11 Late Tertiary	EVENTS: By this time, tensional faulting again penetrated into the more rigid continental interior. Eruption of basalt (25) resumed in the Glenwood Springs area. Aspen's climate at this time was that of a semiarid steppe, supporting an oak-juniper-grass vegetation and a fauna that included horse, camel, rhinoceros, and antelope. The average land elevation was probably between 3000 and 5000 feet.
12.5 Late Tertiary	EVENTS: Granite (26) was intruded in the Treasure Mountain Dome on the western edge of the Elk Mountain gravity glide sheet. About 5000 feet of local uplift occurred there at that time, and the Grand Hogback monocline was further warped upward to the east, fracturing basalt flows that had been erupted over the monocline a short time beforehand.
12.5 Upper Tertiary	ROCK UNIT 26: *Treasure Mountain Granite*. Pink to gray granite. Probably derived from local melting of the continental crust at moderate depth. Best seen on the road between Crystal and Marble.

11-0 Upper Tertiary/ Quaternary	**UPLIFT, GLACIATION, AND CANYON-CUTTING**
11-10 Late Tertiary	EVENTS: A major, regional uplift took place, with more basaltic volcanism in the Aspen area. This, apparently, was the event that created the Colorado River. Up to this time, precipitation in the southwestern United States had been too slight to generate and maintain a major, throughgoing river with an outlet to the sea. Streams flowing from mountain regions had terminated in playa lakes or desert alluvial fans. But now, the land was elevated sufficiently to intercept the high-level, moist, westerly winds. Precipitation increased markedly in the highlands, and newly formed perennial streams, including the Roaring Fork, quickly organized themselves into a major drainage system, the Colorado River, flowing through Arizona's Grand Canyon to the Gulf of California. The earliest certain evidence for the existence of the Colorado River is in the river gravels deposited on an 11- to 10-million-year-old basalt flow on a mesa top near Glenwood Springs. The young drainage system found itself flowing over a rugged and uneven terrain at first. By cutting and filling its bed, it gradually produced a channel profile that would serve most efficiently to move rain water and sediment from the land. This was accomplished mainly by waterfalls migrating upstream from the sea, cutting deep canyons in the process. Eventually, a smoothly graded channel profile became established throughout the mainstream and the various tributaries of the Colorado River drainage. Canyons of varying narrowness and depth were formed wherever the drainage system cut down below the old Rocky Mountain erosion surface.
8.8 Late Tertiary	EVENT: The shield volcano of Basalt Mountain erupted, eighteen miles northwest of Aspen, spilling basaltic lava onto the Rocky Mountain erosion surface. The Roaring Fork canyon cuts

through these lavas, indicating that the canyon had not yet formed at the time of the eruption.

8.8-7.9
Late
Tertiary

EVENT: A broad valley, about 2000 feet deep, was cut by the Roaring Fork River below the Rocky Mountain erosion surface during this interval. Eastward, toward Aspen and the hard, crystalline rocks of the Sawatch Range, the valley became shallower: about 1500 feet below the Rocky Mountain erosion surface, judging by a remnant of the broad valley surface on the west slope of Red Mountain (above the flat glacial outwash terraces). The flat tops of Red and Smuggler mountains, north and east of Aspen, are parts of the Rocky Mountain erosion surface. Independence Pass, thirteen miles to the east and about 2000 feet higher, is another. Beyond the Continental Divide, the surface descends again eastward, until it eventually blends with the Great Plains.

7.9
Late
Tertiary

EVENT: A second eruption, just west of the town of Basalt, spilled basalt lava onto the broad valley surface of the Roaring Fork, thereby fixing a minimum age for the cutting of the broad valley.

8-1.5
Late
Tertiary/
Quaternary

EVENTS: Ongoing regional uplift of the western United States brought the land surface increasingly into colder regions of the atmosphere, thereby allowing snow to accumulate on the highlands. As accumulation exceeded ablation (melting and evaporation) an ice cap formed on the Rocky Mountain erosion surface along the Continental Divide. The peaks, rising 1000 or 2000 feet above the erosion surface, probably weren't submerged in the ice. Bouldery moraine (27) from the ice cap is present both on the Rocky Mountain erosion surface on the tops of Red and Smuggler mountains and on the broad valley surface on Red Mountain. Outwash gravel deposits (28) on ridgetops representing the broad valley surface west of Aspen, and on the Rocky Mountain erosion surface northwest of Aspen, show that the glacier didn't extend more than about thirteen miles west of the Continental Divide (see the geologic map).

3? Quaternary	At Deadman Pass in the Sierra Nevada of California, moraine of a similar ice cap glaciation is sandwiched between two lava flows dated radiometrically at 3.1 and 2.7 million years old. If this Californian glaciation was contemporaneous with the one at Aspen, then the latter may also be about 3 million years old. ROCK UNIT 27: *Ice Cap glacial moraine.* Unlayered, unsorted, unlithified mixture of rounded boulders, cobbles, gravel, sand, silt, and clay. Rock material transported and abraded beneath an ice sheet. Occurs only on ridgetops and flat surfaces above 8400 feet elevation. Best seen on top of Red Mountain.
2.5? Quaternary	ROCK UNIT 28: *Ice Cap glacial outwash.* Roughly layered and sorted, unlithified mixture of rounded cobbles, gravel, and sand with minor silt and boulders. Moraine material washed away from a glacier margin by meltwater streams. Best seen capping a ridge on the southeast side of Highway 82, east of the town of Basalt.
1.5 Quaternary	EVENT: A small basalt flow (29) was erupted on top of Ice Cap outwash gravel on the broad valley surface fourteen miles northwest of Aspen near Woody Creek. This gives a minimum age for the Ice Cap glaciation. The eruption took place along the Castle Creek fault zone, which runs from Basalt southeastward to Aspen, and then south along the Castle Creek valley. South of Aspen, this fault coincides with the line along which the rocks of the Sawatch Range have been uplifted as much as 26,000 feet above the country to the west over the past 70 million years.
1.5 Quaternary	ROCK UNIT 29: *Younger basalt.* Like 26. Best seen in a hill on the north side of the Woody Creek road, about one mile northwest of the town of Woody Creek.
1.5-0 Quaternary	EVENTS: The present narrow gorge of the Roaring Fork River was cut as much as 1600 feet below the broad valley surface, probably due in part to

regional uplift at the time of the 1.5-million-year-old basalt eruption, and in part to fluctuations in climate, vegetation and streamflow caused by a series of glaciations that began at some time since that eruption. These later glaciations, unlike the first, have been confined to valleys whose walls have been scoured into a broad U shape by the passage of glacial ice.

So far, four different glaciations have been identified, each with its moraine (30) and outwash gravel (31), but many more may have occurred for which the record was obscured or obliterated by later glaciations. Of these four, the first two were the most extensive, and the fourth, or last, the least extensive. The town of Aspen sits on outwash gravel of the Third Valley glaciation at its junction with terminal moraine of the same age.

In Wyoming's Wind River Range, and at several other places in the Rocky Mountains, a similar sequence of four valley glaciations following an ice cap glaciation has been identified. The ice cap glaciation has been named the Buffalo, and the valley glaciations the Early and Late Bull Lake and the Early and Late Pinedale. Recent dating of obsidian from glacial moraine in Yellowstone Park indicates ages of 130,000 to 110,000 years for the Bull Lake glaciers and 40,000 to 30,000 years for the Pinedale. The sequence and the ages of the Aspen glacial deposits may or may not be the same as those of the Wind River Range, but the similarities are compelling. We have designated the five Aspen glaciations identified so far as the Ice Cap, the Oldest Valley, the Second Valley, the Third Valley and the Youngest Valley glaciations.

Why glaciation is cyclic is a much-debated issue. Currently, the hypothesis that seems to be most in vogue is one that invokes periodic changes in the energy output of the Sun acting in combination with cyclic variations in the Earth's orbit and axial tilt. The stage for glaciation was set by the general, broad uplift of the western United States, which placed the land surface at a high enough elevation that more snow could accumulate in winter than would melt in summer, given the appropriate climatic conditions.

Although the term *Holocene,* or *Recent,* was coined years ago to designate the time interval since the last glaciation, with the implication that it was, indeed, the *last* glaciation, with none to follow, there now seems to be no reason to believe that glaciation is strictly a thing of the past. On the contrary, there seems to be every reason to expect a return of glacial ice to Canada and the Rocky Mountains at some indefinite time in the future, since the environmental conditions under which glaciation occurred in the past are still with us.

Meanwhile, various geological processes are at work in the Aspen area which are modifying the characteristic, smooth, U-shaped valleys of a glaciated mountain range. Rockfalls, landslides, and mudflows (32) are removing material from the upper parts of glacially oversteepened valley walls and depositing them on their lower slopes. Streams are cutting new channels through glacial moraine and underlying bedrock ridges, and depositing alluvial mud, sand, and gravel (33) in floodplains. Now and then, a healthy earthquake reminds Aspenites that the tectonic proclivities of this high mountain region are far from extinct.

1.5-0 Quaternary
ROCK UNIT 30: *Valley glacial moraine.* Like 27, but restricted in occurrence to valleys and their sideslopes. Best seen along the Rio Grande Trail.

1.5-0 Quaternary
ROCK UNIT 31: *Valley glacial outwash.* Like 28, but restricted in occurrence to valleys. Best seen along Woody Creek Road southeast of the town of Woody Creek, where four successively younger outwash units (the Oldest Valley, the Second Valley, the Third Valley and the Youngest Valley) form four successively lower terraces above the present floodplain of the Roaring Fork River.

.012-0 Quaternary
ROCK UNIT 32: *Landslide deposits.* Unlayered, unsorted, unlithified mixture of (usually) angular boulders, cobbles, gravel, sand, silt, and minor clay. Common on steep valley sideslopes. Best seen

.012-0
Quaternary

in roadcuts along Maroon Creek Road.

ROCK UNIT 33: *Alluvium.* Layered, sorted, unlithified deposits of gravel, sand, and silt. River flood deposits. Restricted to valley flats. Best seen in the flat meadows in the Roaring Fork Valley just east of Aspen.

Road and Trail Logs

How To Use the Logs

Probably the first question that will arise is, "Which should be done first?" We've arranged the logs in an order that's designed to answer that question, but the order is only suggestive. Each trip has its own unique and fascinating features, and each stands on its own as a complete experience. The logs we've placed first are ones that we feel present somewhat more of an overall view, while the later ones tend to give more intimate pictures of certain aspects of geology in the Aspen area.

The five roads and six trails are shown on the geologic map inside the back cover and, in more detail, on the topographic maps that follow the logs. Certain roads and trails may most conveniently be taken together on the same outing, as we've shown below, if you allow sufficient time to do both a road and trail in the same day, or if you go prepared to camp.

Roads and Trails That May Be Done Together

Road	**Trail**
Independence Pass ½ day	Independence Lake ½ day
Lincoln Creek ¼ day	Grizzly Lake 1 day
Maroon Creek ¼ day	Buckskin Pass 1 day

Mileages are given for the various stops on the road logs. Read your odometer at the starting point of the trip, and then add the number of miles shown for each stop to your starting mileage. If you overshoot and have to backtrack to a stop, just add in the extra mileage to the starting figure and continue as before. If you have a pocket calculator or a shopper's price adder, you may want to take it along to simplify the figuring. Of course, mileages aren't given for the stops on the trail logs. These are identified by their sequence and by distinctive features.

A number in parentheses will usually follow a mention of a rock unit, e.g., "The Morrison Formation (16) consists of..." etc. In this case, you would refer to the sixteenth rock unit listed in *The Geological Setting* for a concise description of the Morrison Formation and its origins.

Road Logs

Independence Pass Road

Colorado State Highway 82; ½ day, 20.5 miles, elevation gain 4188 feet from Aspen, at 7907 feet to Independence Pass, at 12,095 feet.

USGS Topographic Quadrangle Maps: Aspen, Thimble Rock, New York Peak and Independence Pass.
USGS Geologic Quadrangle Maps: Aspen GQ-933.

0.00 *Start at the Jerome Hotel on the corner of Main and Mill streets in Aspen, and drive east.*

The flat surface on which the town of Aspen was built is a glacial outwash plain (31). Meltwater from the Third Valley glacier, which advanced down the valley of the Roaring Fork River, carried sand, gravel and boulders away from the glacier as it melted, and deposited them farther downvalley at and below the townsite of Aspen.

To the east of the town, Smuggler Mountain marks the western edge of the great Sawatch Range, uplifted in several pulses during the last 72 million years (Plate 6A). The granitic rock (3) of Smuggler Mountain is 1.47 billion years old. Younger sedimentary rocks (4-10) rest on the western slope of Smuggler, turned up sharply on the flank of the Sawatch uplift. Many of the richest silver mines of the Aspen district were worked in these younger rocks. Mine roads and dumps are still visible on Smuggler's west slope. Glacial moraine (30) covers the lower portion of the slope where the Second Valley glacier, more extensive than the Third, plastered rock debris against the Roaring Fork Valley walls.

To the south, Ajax, or Aspen Mountain, dominates the town with its massive north slope, bedecked with ski lifts and trails (Plate 1A). This mountain is also composed of the same ancient granite (3), but the younger rocks—sandstones, limestones and shales (4-10)—are better preserved here than on Smuggler Mountain. Aspen Mountain is broken by a complex array of faults, and the sedimentary rocks have been protected from erosion in downdropped blocks among the fault planes. Between 72 and 67 million years ago, porphyry sills (21) were injected into the sediments before the faulting. These porphyries brought lead, zinc and silver minerals with them to form part of the rich deposits that made the town of Aspen so prosperous in the late 1800's.

The bright red rocks of Red Mountain, north of Aspen, give this long, flat-topped peak its name (Plate 1B). This mixed deposit of red shale and sandstone, the Maroon Formation (12), is younger than the sediments on Smuggler and Aspen mountains, but older than the porphyries. It was deposited in a deep, narrow seaway between two high mountain ranges, the Ancestral Rocky Mountains, which began to rise about 300 million years ago. The red sediments are the product of rapid erosion of these high mountains under a very hot, dry climate punctuated by tropical hurricanes and flash floods. It has a maximum thickness of more than two miles.

The flattish tops of both Red and Smuggler mountains are remnants of an old erosion surface, called the Rocky Mountain surface, which was formed during a period of geologic stability in the Earth's crust between about 57 and 36 million years ago. The surface rises over 2000 feet to a crest a few miles east of Independence Pass, and then falls again until it blends with the Great Plains. Subsequent uplift and erosion has dissected the Rocky Mountain surface with deep canyons like that of the Roaring Fork.

0.70 *Bridge over the Roaring Fork River at the east end of town*

Here, the Roaring Fork has cut its bed about twelve feet below the Second Valley glacial outwash plain (31). The large, rounded boulders in the riverbed were washed out of Third Valley glacial moraine (30) upriver. Their presence here shows that the river is still downcutting. When rivers have cut downward to their base levels, they tend to develop smooth, sandy or muddy channels. The boulders are composed of 1- to 2-billion-year-old gneiss and granite of the Sawatch Range (1 and 3).

Just beyond the bridge, the highway rises through a roadcut in a bank of hummocky Third Valley glacial moraine (30). This is the terminal moraine of the next to the last glacier that flowed down the Roaring Fork Valley. Its location shows that the glacier "stopped" at this point. More precisely, this was the place where glacial advance was exactly balanced by melting. Consequently, all the rock debris being transported by the glacier was dumped at this point. Notice how heterogeneous this deposit is: huge boulders are indiscriminately intermingled with cobbles, gravel, sand, silt, and clay, and no hint of stratification, or layering, is present. These characteristics, plus the rounded boulders and hummocky topography, serve to identify glacial moraine.

1.85 *Small pullout on right opposite a prominent cutbank on left*

Here, the granite of the steep south slope of Smuggler Mountain, oversteepened by the passage of several generations of valley glaciers, has been covered by landslide debris. This deposit resembles glacial moraine in being unstratified and in having a wide range of particle sizes from clay to boulders, but most of the fragments here are angular, while those in moraine tend to be more rounded.

The Roaring Fork River, south of the highway, meanders over a flat floodplain (Plate 2A), and its bed is composed of sand and mud. After the melting of the glacier that formed the terminal moraine you have just driven across, a large lake filled the valley behind the natural dam of the moraine. In time, the lake became filled in with sand, silt and mud (33), which underlie the present floodplain. Notice the hummocky terrain of the moraine surface to the south and west, contrasting with the level land of the floodplain.

4.30 *Entrance to Difficult Campground*

The narrow valley on the mountainside across the road served as the channelway for a large mud flow (32), the debris from which now forms a broad, fan-shaped deposit extending out from the mountain slope into the valley. This mudflow deposit differs from glacial moraine in having a narrower range of particle sizes (few large boulders and little fine clay) and in being crudely stratified.

5.05 *Large pullout on right on a long upgrade*

From here, looking east, you can see a large, low, forested mound filling most of the valley bottom to the east. This is the terminal moraine of the Youngest Valley glacier, which descended the Roaring Fork Valley down to this point.

The deep, narrow valley of the Roaring Fork has been cut by stream and glacial erosion within the past 1.5 million years, following a regional uplift of the land. This uplift has been dated by a lava flow of that age on a higher valley surface near Woody Creek.

Here, in the resistant granite of the Sawatch Range east of Aspen, the Roaring Fork Valley is considerably deeper and narrower than it is to the west of Aspen, where the bedrock is softer and more easily eroded. Part of this added depth is due to the action of at least four valley glaciers.

5.55 *U.S. Forest Service life zone signs in pullout*

The small creek across the road from you separates moraine of the Third Valley glaciation on the west from that of the Youngest Valley glaciation on the east. The presence of the Youngest Valley terminal moraine accounts for the steepening of the valley floor here and the need for this long upgrade to bring the highway above it.

The roadcut ahead is made through a mudflow fan. A fairly fresh rockslide (32) can be seen at the east end of the roadcut. Moderate lichen cover and sparse vegetation indicate that the slide is fairly recent. The canyon opposite the pullout lies along a major fault which dropped the country on the west side an unknown amount.

6.15 *Pullout on right; small lake and horse pasture to right*

The situation here is equivalent to that at the 1.85 mile stop, with floodplain deposits filling in behind the Youngest Valley terminal moraine.

7.35 *Pullout on right in aspen forest*

North of the road, the hummocky and bouldery terrain is typical of young glacial moraine.

8.25 *Pullout on right opposite rock buttress*

This buttress marks the beginning of a major change in rock type. Between here and Aspen, you have been driving through 1.47-billion-year-old quartz monzonite (3), a gray, granitic, igneous rock. East of here, the Roaring Fork Valley is cut in biotite gneiss (1). This metamorphic rock was originally a great thickness of graywacke, deposited as mud, impure sand and volcanic debris in an offshore trench about 1.9 billion years ago. With the intrusion of the quartz monzonite and an earlier granodiorite (2), about 1.7 billion years ago, these sediments were metamorphosed to banded gneisses.

Several dark inclusions of gneiss appear in the lighter igneous rock of the buttress. These were broken off the wallrocks by the upwelling granitic magma and partially digested. Rusty, mineralized faults run through the buttress in a northerly direction. One on the right has been extensively weathered out where the rock has been fractured and altered by hot water solutions circulating through the fractures. The presence of the faults and the change in rock type appear to have been responsible for the sharp bend in the Roaring Fork River at this point and for the steepening of the gradient of the river bed.

Beyond the buttress, the highway is cut through the toe of a large rockfall. Notice the large, angular boulders which fell from a prominent cliff to the north. The cliff will become visible beyond the next left turn.

To the south, a hanging glacial valley enters the Roaring Fork canyon. A small tributary glacier descended this valley from New York Peak to join the main glacier in the Roaring Fork. The floor of the hanging valley is higher than that of the main valley because the latter was more extensively deepened by the larger glacier(s) flowing within it.

8.70 *Weller Campground*

The cliff behind the campground is the source of the rockfall debris just mentioned (Plate 2B). The metamorphic rocks forming the canyon walls east of Weller Campground are banded biotite gneiss (1). Since this rock type is more resistant to erosion than is the igneous quartz monzonite (3) to the west, the canyon is somewhat narrower and its walls somewhat steeper than to the west of the campground.

9.40 *Devil's Punchbowl; pullout on left (*Caution! *Blind curve ahead. You may be able to get into a smaller pullout on the right, just before this one.)*

Here, the Roaring Fork River has cut its channel down through the bedrock, creating a picturesque pattern of watersculptured forms. Little gorges like this, and some larger ones, are characteristic of glaciated terrain where streams, reestablishing themselves after the melting of the glaciers, cut their way down to bedrock through a blanket of glacial moraine. Rarely do the streams find their old channels. Where a stream encounters a ridge of bedrock in its downcutting, as happened here, it scours its way down through the obstacle, aided by an ample supply of sand and gravel from the moraine.

9.65 *Access road on right to the old Grottoes Campground (subtract 0.10 mile from subsequent mileages if you don't drive in). Park in the lot at the end of the access road. Walk through the meadow to the west to a large rock outcrop with trees on it.*

The rock is a mixture of biotite gneiss (1) and quartz monzonite (3). The latter intruded the former in a molten state 1.47 billion years ago. These rocks were in the vicinity of the contact zone where granitic magma forced its way into the surrounding gneiss along planes of weakness.

The outcrop has a smooth, rounded surface. This is an indication of glacial scour. If you walk up on the outcrop, notice the long, deep grooves in its upper surface where boulders embedded in the base of the glacier scoured out weaker rock. On the downvalley end, the rounded surface is broken abruptly by steep cliffs where the moving glacier plucked large blocks away from the outcrop.

From the parking lot, cross the footbridge over the Roaring Fork River.

To the left of the trail is a broad area of glacially scoured and grooved quartz monzonite bedrock (3). Sitting on top of the smoothed bedrock are large, rounded granite boulders, one of which rests in a pothole that was probably scoured out by glacial meltwater (Plate 3A). These boulders were being transported down the valley by the Youngest Valley glacier. When the climate warmed up enough that the advancing edge of the glacier was melting faster than new snow could replenish the supply of ice at the head of the valley, the glacier began to shrink. Eventually, it stopped flowing altogether when it had been reduced to a certain size. Boulders trapped in the stagnant ice were then let down upon the ground beneath as the ice melted. Many of these *glacial erratics* were perched in highly improbable places, as here.

About 200 feet farther on, the trail crosses a large quartz vein, about eight inches across, cutting through the granitic bedrock. Quartz is very soluble in superheated water. Igneous magma, rising from deep within the Earth's crust, contains a small amount of water, and it picks up more as it ascends through the overlying rocks. This water becomes concentrated as the magma crystallizes because there is no place for water in the crystal structure of the minerals that make up granite except for biotite and amphibole, which are present only in small amounts. So, the excess water separates out of the magma and soaks up large amounts of quartz. This quartz solution may then be injected into cracks that develop in the overlying country rock, as here.

Frequently, other substances that don't fit in granitic mineral crystals are also concentrated in this residual water, including gold and sulfides of lead, zinc, silver, copper and iron. These are deposited along with quartz, and they often make valuable ore deposits, as in the Aspen mining district.

In a trailcut in bedrock about 50 feet ahead on the right there is a small body of pink *pegmatite*, a very coarse form of granite in which the individual crystals are unusually large due to a high water content in the cooling magma. The pink mineral is *orthoclase*, or potassium feldspar, and the white one is quartz.

In 1954, C.B. Hunt described an igneous intrusive he found as a "quasi-horizontal chonolith composed of anastomosing ductoliths whose distal ends curl like a harpolith, thin like a sphenolith or bulge discordantly like an akmolith or ethmolith." (Learn this, and amaze your friends.) He called it a *cactolith* for short, because it looked rather like a cactus. No one seems to be quite sure what a cactolith really is, but this pegmatite body may qualify. A less imaginative definition might be "an irregularly shaped intrusive."

The deep, narrow gorge in quartz monzonite (3) on the left was formed at the margin of a stagnant, melting glacier when meltwater, rushing downvalley along the edge of the ice, scoured out a deep groove in the bedrock. Large blocks of rock have been broken away from the walls of this meltwater channel in its eastern end. A "whaleback" ridge lies between the channel and the trail (Plate 3B). This glacially smoothed granite ridge has a large quartz vein on its crest. On its east end, two sets of intersecting joints or fractures may be seen. All the joints of each set are parallel to each other, and because of this regularity, geologists can actually reconstruct the forces that affected a particular area by studying the attitudes of a large number of joint planes such as these.

The trail continues for about 300 yards to the confluence of Lincoln Creek and the Roaring Fork. Return to the large clearing opposite the pink pegmatite cactolith, and walk down the scoured bedrock surface, keeping right, until you come to a very narrow, deep, winding gorge.

This water-sculpted slot canyon (Plate 4A) is the downvalley extension of the wider, straighter ice-margin meltwater channel you saw farther up the trail. Unlike that channel, however, this one has a small stream flowing in it. The stream enters the channel from the south side in the woods to the east. Probably, a blanket of glacial moraine was left here at the end of the last glaciation. The little stream cut down through the moraine and on down through the bedrock beneath it, forming this bizarre, contorted gorge. Ice may remain in the bottom of the gorge throughout the year.

Return to your vehicle and drive back up to Highway 82.

10.10 *Sharp bend in the road and in the river*

For the next several hundred yards, abundant rockfall deposits of biotite gneiss (1) are present on the steep north wall of the canyon. Rockfalls are common in mountain areas where valley glaciers have oversteepened the valley walls, as here.

10.80 *Lincoln Creek roadhead (see the log for Lincoln Creek Road)*

12.05 *Nearly level ground*

While unglaciated valleys tend to have rather smooth longitudinal profiles, glacial erosion often produces a "stairstep" effect with level "treads" on more easily erodible rock and steep "risers" on more resistant rock. The tread here is thinly covered by a deposit of ground moraine.

12.85 *Pullout on right*

The young aspens growing on the rockslide across the road must be younger than the slide. They might be used to determine a minimum age of the rockslide by obtaining tree ring counts. A special instrument, the Swedish increment borer, may be used to remove a thin core from a tree for ring counting.

13.00 *Pullout on right*

On the north slope of Green Mountain, across the river, is a major avalanche path (Plate 4B). Snow avalanches originate in the shallow bowl above timberline, or in the chutes above it, and sweep down through the spruce-fir forest to the valley floor. The central portion of the slide is kept clear of trees by the frequent avalanches, but young trees are present in narrow belts bordering the slide path. Eventually, these young trees will also be removed by the largest avalanche possible on this slope, a rather infrequent, but inevitable, event. Willow, aspen, grass and herbs grow in the center of the slide path.

At the base of the path is a large *talus fan* composed of rock debris that has slid down the avalanche track during spring and summer. Green Mountain is made of the same 1.47-billion-year-old quartz monzonite (3) as Smuggler Mountain northeast of Aspen.

14.45 *Trailhead on left*

14.65 *Lostman Campground on right*

The broad, glaciated valley of Lost Man Creek enters the Roaring Fork Valley from the north at this point. Floodplain deposits have built up in the lower reaches of Lost Man Valley. These are covered by dense willow thickets.

15.20 *Pullout on right*

Independence Mountain, ahead, has a distinctly different appearance from the granitic and gneissic mountains farther down the valley. Its slopes are steeper, less vegetated, and more reddish-gray in color, with more abundant talus fans and cones and rockslide gullies. The mountains to the west have gentler slopes with less talus and more vegetation. They appear to be (and are) harder and more resistant to erosion.

Independence Mountain is on the north edge of the Grizzly caldera, a volcanic vent nine miles in diameter that erupted first quietly and then violently about 34 million years ago. The mountain has been carved by stream and glacial erosion from the widespread, hot-welded volcanic ash flow deposits (24) from these eruptions.

15.85 *Pullout on right*

But for frequent snow avalanches, the slopes across the valley would be heavily forested. Most of the Rocky Mountain wildflower meadows in the Subalpine zone below timberline are maintained in their treeless condition by snow avalanches.

A tributary valley enters the Roaring Fork a short distance downriver. At the mouth of the tributary is a broad, low alluvial fan built up by mudflows. The Roaring Fork River has cut through the toe of the fan, showing that such mudflows occasionally dam the Roaring Fork by depositing debris across the channel.

16.35 *Independence Townsite overlook*

The hewn log buildings of the old mining camp of Independence are sitting on the toe of a landslide, which appears as a large, hummocky lobe on the north wall of the valley. The floodplain of the Roaring Fork has cut into the slide toe at its lower end. On the opposite slope, the valley of Independence Creek enters that of the Roaring Fork through a narrow notch cut through both glacial moraine and bedrock. As often happens, the Roaring Fork glacier deepened the valley floor somewhat more than the smaller glacier in Independence Creek deepened that valley. After the glaciers melted and the two streams were reestablished in their valleys, Independence Creek entered the Roaring Fork by a waterfall. Gradually, the waterfall has cut back up the creek, forming the narrow notch. A large avalanche track on Independence Mountain enters the notch from the right.

Gold lured the founders of Independence to this inhospitable site in 1879. The discovery of the Independence lode occurred on the 4th of July of that year. In its heyday, the town had a population of about 2000, but this dwindled rapidly after the high grade ore became depleted around 1900. Probably, the gold mineralization was related to the activity of the Grizzly caldera about 34 million years ago.

16.85 *Pullout on right opposite gully on left*

This gully is not an avalanche path but a snowmelt flood channel. The small Lodgepole pines in the channel are able to withstand the minor spring floods, but they wouldn't survive a snow avalanche. South-facing slopes rarely have large avalanches, because the Sun tends to stabilize the snow on southern exposures.

18.35 *Pullout on right*

Across the valley, the glacially oversteepened wall is broken by gullies in its upper part and filled by talus from the gullies at the base. Here, erosion and gravity are gradually working to reduce the steep valley wall to a gentler angle.

18.75 *Pullout on left at hairpin turn and Roaring Fork River sign. See Independence Lake log, which begins here.*

19.40 *Pullout on right*

This is an excellent vantage point from which to view the classic U-shaped cross-profile of a glaciated valley with its oversteepened walls (Plate 5A). Notice the irregular *meander scars* surrounding the Roaring Fork River channel. These mark former positions of the channel, which winds back and forth on the floodplain, shifting its position from time to time, whenever a major flood occurs. This stretch of the river is on a flattish "stair tread" cut in quartz monzonite (3) and Grizzly Ash-flow Tuff (24). Farther downstream the tread, and the floodplain, end at a "riser" of more resistant biotite gneiss (1) where the river steepens again and has rapids instead of meander bends.

The gently rolling bench that forms the left and right skyline above the glacial valley and below the highest peaks is the same surface that forms the summits of Red and Smuggler mountains at Aspen (see Plate 6A), but here it's about 2000 feet higher. This is the Rocky Mountain erosion surface, formed mainly between 57 and 36 million years ago. This surface originally blended with the Great Plains before the latest episode of regional uplift of the Rocky Mountain region that began about 10 million years ago. Since then, rivers and glaciers have cut deep canyons below that old surface to create the impressive mountain scenery of the region today. It seems a bit odd, perhaps, that what gives the Rockies their magnificence is more a matter of *canyons* than of mountains, but this is actually the case.

20.65 *Independence Pass*

This is a saddle on the Continental Divide, slightly below the level of the Rocky Mountain erosion surface. To the east, rivers drain to the Atlantic Ocean; to the west, they drain to the Pacific. The north side of the pass, including Blue Mountain, is cut in 1.47-billion-year-old quartz monzonite (3), while the south side is in older (1.7 billion years) granodiorite (2). On the southeast side of the pass, the double glacial valley of Mountain Boy Gulch can be seen. Here, glaciers have scoured a split-level valley below the Rocky Mountain erosion surface (the deeper, narrower valley is the younger). The shoulder above the deeper valley is called an *alp* (see Plate 21B). The same feature gives the Alps of Europe their name.

Castle Creek Road

½ day, 14 miles; elevation gain about 1900 feet from Aspen, at 7907 feet to Pitkin County Iron Mine gate at about 9800 feet.

0.00 *Castle Creek Roadhead. For access, see Maroon Creek log*

Due south of the intersection is Highland Peak, with the ski trails of the Aspen Highlands Ski Area on its slopes (Plate 5B). The summit is composed of red shale and sandstone of the Maroon Formation (12) derived from the erosion of the Ancestral Rocky

Mountains between about 293 and 270 million years ago. These sediments, and those above and below them, were originally flat-lying, but they now dip to the north (toward you) at about 20 to 30 degrees on the north slope of the Elk Range.

This range, and its adjacent eastern neighbor, the Sawatch Range, both came into existence at the same time, about 72 to 67 million years ago. A powerful uplift took place along a north-south belt immediately east of Aspen, raising the Sawatch Mountains. The west flank of this uplift was evidently steep enough that most of the great blanket of overlying sedimentary rocks slid westward off the rising Sawatch Range under the influence of gravity. This spectacular landslide involved a sheet of rock that probably measured 20 by 50 miles in area and up to 5 miles in thickness. The sheet slid upon a basal glide plane within the soft, limy shales of the Belden Formation (9). On its western edge, south of Snowmass Mountain, the sedimentary layers against which it slid have been thrown into a huge overturned fold, the Schofield syncline. The syncline was breached on its upper limb, and the landslide sheet rode westward beyond it for an undetermined distance, but this extension has since been eroded away.

About 34 million years ago, granodiorite magma (22) was injected into the Elk Range, especially along the basal glide plane, further elevating the mountains.

The main ski slope in the foreground, with a ski lift angling across it, is Third Valley glacial moraine (30) on the left, and red Chinle shale (14) on the right. The large, forested hill extending left from the ski hill is the recessional moraine of a Third Valley glacier, which descended the Castle Creek Valley. The rock debris that was being transported by the moving glacier was dumped at this spot during a temporary halt in the upvalley retreat of the glacier at the end of the glacial episode.

The flat surface on which the Aspen Chapel is built is ground moraine of the same glaciation deposited beneath the ice when it was somewhat farther downvalley. The lower flat surface that you are on is glacial outwash (31) deposited by streams flowing away from the melting glacier terminus and down into the Roaring Fork. The town of Aspen is built on the same surface. The Castle Creek Valley extends southward to the left of the chapel.

East of Castle Creek is the steep west slope of Ajax, or Aspen Mountain. The lower portions of this slope consist of 1.47-billion-year-old quartz monzonite (3), a granitic intrusive rock. To the east of the Castle Creek Valley, within the high terrain of the Sawatch Range, this rock type prevails to and beyond the

Continental Divide. The Castle Creek fault zone, a major break in the Earth's crust, downthrown to the west, separates these older granites from the younger, sedimentary rocks that make up the terrain west of Castle Creek. These sediments once extended eastward over the Sawatch Range, but since the uplift of that range, about 70 million years ago, they have been removed from it by erosion and by the gravity-gliding mentioned above.

The easternmost remnants of the former sedimentary cover in the Sawatch Range are on the summit of Ajax Mountain. The north end of the west ridge of Ajax is veneered with three of the oldest sedimentary formations (4, 5 and 6), about half a billion years old. They have been tilted up from their originally horizontal attitude by a succession of uplifts of the Sawatch Range that began 72 million years ago, so that now they dip at about 55 degrees north-northwest.

To the east is the broad, flat-topped mass of Smuggler Mountain which, like Ajax, is composed of quartz monzonite (3) (Plate 6A). Red Mountain, to the northeast, is also flat-topped, and is composed of red shales and sandstones of the Maroon Formation (Plate 1B). A sharp bend in the Earth's crust lies between the two mountains where the Hunter Creek Valley comes down to the Roaring Fork. This bend defines the western edge of the Sawatch Range uplift east of Aspen.

Curiously, both Smuggler and Red mountains are "mountains" only in a negative sense. Their flat summits are remnants of the Rocky Mountain erosion surface, a plain of low relief developed extensively in the western interior during a geologically inactive period between about 57 and 36 million years ago. When the entire Rocky Mountain region was broadly uplifted by several thousand feet about 10 million years ago, the Roaring Fork and other tributaries of the Colorado River system began to cut deep canyons below the old land surface, a process that is still going on. Apparently, the Colorado River system didn't exist before this major uplift.

The valley of Hunter Creek is a *hanging glacial valley*, which is to say that the series of glaciers that flowed in it failed to deepen the valley as much as the glaciers in the Roaring Fork did to their valley. This explains the sudden steep drop of Hunter Creek at its lower end.

The prominent terrace at the base of Red Mountain is ground moraine of the Second Valley glaciation (Plate 12A, behind Red Butte). The glacier that left this older moraine extended farther down the Roaring Fork Valley than more recent ones, and its moraine can be traced as far as the Aspen airport. Above this terrace are two obscure irrigation ditches. They appear to slant up slightly to the west, an illusion created by the greater westward slope of the Roaring Fork Valley. Actually, they, too, slope very gently westward. Both are in a poorly preserved higher terrace remnant of the Oldest Valley moraine.

On the summits of Red and Smuggler mountains, a different kind of glacial moraine (27) is present. Unlike those previously mentioned, this one appears to have been laid down by a broad ice sheet that flowed outward from the Continental Divide upon the Rocky Mountain erosion surface after the regional uplift but before the deep valleys had been cut.

On the western slope of Red Mountain is a roughly level area nearly a thousand feet below the summit and a thousand feet above the highest, Oldest Valley glacial outwash terrace at the base of the mountain (Plate 1B, left). This is a remnant of a broad valley surface cut below the Rocky Mountain erosion surface by the Roaring Fork and its tributaries between 9 and 8 million years ago. Ice sheet moraine is also present on this broad valley surface, showing that the ice cap glaciation occurred after the broad valley was cut. But in the deep gorges that have been cut below the broad valley surface within the last 1.5 million years, ice cap moraine is absent. This suggests that the cutting of these gorges, initiated by a broad, regional uplift 1.5 million years ago, took place after the ice cap glaciation was over.

Red Butte, to the north (Plate 12A), is a large block of rocks that has been caught between two major faults in the Castle Creek fault zone and rotated so that the sedimentary rock formations in the block have been turned past the vertical and are now upside down.

Red Butte was formerly the southern end of a long ridge extending southward from Red Mountain. This ridge was buried in Second Valley glacial moraine. When the Roaring Fork River began to flow again, after the glacier melted, it found a new course farther north on the moraine surface above the buried ridge. As the river cut down again toward its old level and beyond, it sawed down through the ridge, thereby cutting off Red Butte.

To the west of Red Butte, two prominent terraces are visible. These are glacial outwash terraces (31) of the Oldest and Second Valley glaciations. The higher of these is the older.

0.65 *Pullout under reddish cutbank on right*

This roadcut exposes the deposits of the recessional moraine mentioned above. Notice the wide range of rock sizes and types: clay to boulders, sandstone to granite. Miscellaneousness is characteristic of glacial moraine.

1.35 *Pullout on left overlooking Aspen Music School*

The deep V-shaped stream valley across Castle Creek is Keno Gulch, which drains the west face of Ajax Mountain (Keno is a Chinese game of chance). About 400 feet above you, hidden by the forest on Ajax, is a major fault along which the country to the east was raised as much as 26,000 feet since the initial uplift of the Sawatch Range about 72 million years ago. This is one branch of the Castle Creek fault zone, which extends northward through Red Butte and southward up the Castle Creek Valley. The slope below the fault is composed of Maroon Formation (12), tilted up beyond the vertical. The upper slope is composed of quartz monzonite (3).

The flattish, aspen-covered bench ahead, to the left of the road, is the terminal moraine of a Youngest Valley glacier, the last to flow down Castle Creek. Red, angular landslide debris appears in the roadcut to the right.

1.50 *Pullout on curve on left*

The outcrop across the road consists of Maroon Formation (12). Here, the originally horizontal beds of fine red sandstone and red and bluish claystone have been overturned in the Castle Creek fault zone so that they now dip 75 degrees, upside down, toward the east. Veins of white, crystalline calcite fill fractures that cut the rock approximately at right angles to the bedding. Such cracks develop especially where rock layers are strongly flexed, as they have been here.

3.00 *Pullout on left opposite red cutbank on right*

The valley of Queens Gulch across Castle Creek is located along a branch fault of the Castle Creek fault zone. Another branch fault passes behind the prominent pinnacle of Maroon Formation on the south side of the valley mouth. The strata in this pinnacle have been turned up at an 80-degree angle. A steep apron of *talus* (rockslide debris) skirts the base of the pinnacle.

On the west side of the road is a cutbank in reddish, semistratified gravel (Cf. Plate 8B). This is an ice-margin feature known as a *kame terrace*. It was formed during the melting of the valley glacier as meltwater flushed moraine material into the growing crevice between the rock wall of the valley and the melting glacier. This washing action tends to sort the moraine material, flushing away the finer clay and mud while leaving the coarser-grained sand and gravel behind in the kame terrace. Red, very angular landslide debris overlies the terrace.

4.05 *Pullout on right by Castle Creek*

The abundance of boulders in the creek bed here indicates that Castle Creek is still cutting downward in this stretch. When rivers reach "grade" and are no longer deepening their valleys, their beds begin to accumulate sand and mud. Here, the creek is cutting down through a composite mass of glacial moraine and landslide material.

To the east, the steep, smooth rock slope is formed on a bedding plane of Maroon siltstone from which overlying, weaker rock and soil have slid away. Slopes like this, formed on bedding planes, are known as *dip slopes*.

Several large blue and Engelmann spruces growing here on the banks of Castle Creek have been undercut by unusually large flood flows. These severe floods can be dated by examining a tree ring core taken with a borer from an undercut and leaning tree. Growth deformities in the annual rings show up first in the ring corresponding to the year in which the flood occurred.

4.95 *Dirt road off to right; pulloff beyond*

The two U-shaped glacial valleys of Castle and Conundrum creeks join here, the latter coming in from the west. To the east is another smaller, fault-controlled valley from which flood debris has flowed out to form an alluvial fan. The road cuts across the fan near its lower end. The dirt road on the left leads up to the Highland Tunnel, which was driven into the mountain in search of ore deposits beneath the old Midnight Mine workings in Annie Basin.

6.00 *Pullout on right on curve*

The nearly vertical beds of purplish tan and mottled fine sandstone across the road belong to the Gothic Formation (10). Originally, the Gothic was deposited as sand and mud in a broad river floodplain to the northeast of the Ancestral Uncompahgre uplift as that large mountain chain began to rise across the southwest corner of Colorado about 300 million years ago. To the east, another major uplift, the Ancestral Front Range, was already in existence at that time, but its greatest development was still to occur some 10 million years later.

Glacial moraine from the Youngest Valley glaciation overlies the outcrop of Gothic Formation.

6.85 *Pullout on right on sagebrush-covered slope*

This is another mudflow fan. From here, you have a good view of Ashcroft Mountain, farther up the valley. On the western slope of Richmond Hill, to the east, sedimentary rocks deposited between 510 million and 290 million years ago (4 through 10) are exposed, now dipping rather steeply westward into rhe Castle Creek fault zone. Seventy- to 67-million-year-old, light-colored intrusive rocks also occur on this slope, cutting the older formations.

7.40 *Pullout on right*

Back about a hundred feet and across the road is a small mine dump. The black rock is from the Belden Formation (9). This is a deposit of oil shale, limestone, and minor sandstone carried southwestward by streams flowing off the rising Ancestral Front Range to the northeast about 310 million years ago. The black color is due to carbon, indicating a swampy, organic-rich but oxygen-poor environment of deposition. When this region was mineralized about 70 million years ago, and again about 34 million years ago, the orebearing fluids had a strong preference for certain layers within the Belden Formation, particularly the highly sheared zone along which the Elk Range gravity glide sheet slid westward off the flank of the rising Sawatch mountain uplift. The eastern edge of the glide sheet, incidentally, is to your right, forming the west wall of Castle Creek canyon. The Gothic Formation (10), which you saw two stops ago, directly overlies the Belden.

9.90 *American Lake trailhead on right; Elk Mountain Lodge cabins on left*

On the mountainside across the creek is an impressive dip slope on the Sawatch Quartzite (4). The material that used to rest on this slope is now below it in a large landslide deposit. This deposit blends with the mudflow fan that you and the Elk Mountain Lodge cabins are standing on. This fan, in turn, overlies a terminal moraine of the Youngest Valley glaciation. Together, the moraine, the fan, and the landslide debris have dammed the valley of Castle Creek, forming a two-mile-long lake, which has by now been completely filled with silt. Beaver ponds are abundant in the willow swamp that now covers the area of the former lake.

11.20 *Ashcroft mining camp*

This old mining town is built on an extensive apron of mudflow deposits from Monument Gulch and Devaney Creek to the west. Across the valley, above a long, basal slope of glacial moraine, the west face of Ashcroft Mountain displays 510- to 345-million-year-old sedimentary rocks (4 through 10) dipping 45 degrees westward along the sharp, faulted flexure that defines the western edge of the Sawatch Range. These sediments were originally deposited in shallow, epicontinental seas that intermittently invaded the Rocky Mountain region from the west.

This sedimentary dipslope on the east wall of the Castle Creek Valley is the source area for the gravity glide sheet that now forms the Elk Range, as we mentioned earlier. The present slope may be somewhat steeper than the one along which the glide sheet slid, some 70 million years ago, since several episodes of uplift have occurred in the Sawatch Range subsequently. Time and erosion have removed several hundred feet of Leadville and Belden strata (8 and 9) from the slope since the great Elk Range slide.

The glide plane itself passes directly through the town of Ashcroft. North of here, it follows, and in fact controls the location of, the Castle Creek Valley, but at Ashcroft, it diverges from Castle Creek and passes up the tributary of Express Creek across the valley from you. Thirty-four million years ago, granodiorite (22) was injected into the Elk Range. Much of this granodiorite followed the zone of weak rock along the basal glide plane. The mineral deposits at Ashcroft, mainly silver, lead and zinc, were worked from 1880 to 1906, when increasing zinc content of the mined ore forced the mines to close.

11.80 *Cathedral Lake trailhead on right*

The U-shaped glacial valley of Pine Creek lies ahead and to the right. The high peaks flanking it are composed of 34-million-year-old intrusive White Rock Granodiorite (22). Some of the peaks to the south, on the Continental Divide, are formed by this same rock, while others are composed of Gothic (10) and Belden (9) formations.

13.90 *Barricade at the Pitkin Iron Corporation mine beyond a a bridge over Castle Creek*

Castle Creek is depositing a rather narrow range of cobble sizes in its bed here. Even-sized particle deposition is a characteristic of streams that have cut down to a stable gradient, and therefore are no longer deepening their channels. High in the mountains, as here, the floods that make such deposits can carry a larger particle size than they do when they reach the lowlands, because here the gradient of the creek bed is much steeper. Gravity assists the floodwaters in moving larger stones down the channel. On gentler slopes, only sand and mud can move under the same rate and volume of floodflow.

Woody Creek Road

¼ day, 10 miles; elevation loss 709 feet from Aspen, at 7909 feet to 7200 feet on the Woody Creek Road.

USGS Topographic Quadrangle Maps: Aspen, Ruedi and Woody Creek.
USGS Geologic Quadrangle Maps: Aspen GQ-933, Ruedi GQ-1004 and Woody Creek GQ-967.

0.00 *From the Jerome Hotel, at Main and Mill streets in Aspen, drive west on Colorado State Highway 82 (Main Street). See the Independence Pass log for a description of the roadhead.*

0.90 *Bridge over Castle Creek*

The bridge spans a 100-foot-deep gorge cut by Castle Creek below the surface of the Third Valley glacial outwash plain (31) on which the town of Aspen is situated. This is a thick gravel deposit laid down by torrential streams rushing away from the next to the last glacier in the Roaring Fork Valley as it melted. Most of the boulders of diverse rock types that line the creek channel here were derived from the outwash deposits. They remain as a *lag concentrate* after floodwater in Castle Creek removed the finer-grained fraction of the outwash.

1.05 *Turn right at stop light onto Cemetery Lane*

1.65 *Pause just before a right bend in the road*

The prominent ridge ahead is Red Butte (Plate 12A). The Earth's crust has been ruptured here along the Castle Creek fault zone, which extends for many miles northwest and south of Aspen. At Red Butte, a block of country within the fault zone was rotated through an angle of 140 degrees so that the originally horizontal sediments are now upside down, dipping northeastward at a 40 degree angle. The country to the east was raised as much as five miles relative to the west side of the fault zone. These enormous shifts have taken place in several pulses of mountain building within the last 70 million years.

1.85 *Top of downgrade*

One might have second thoughts about building a house

at the base of this steep sandstone and shale cliff on Red Butte. The abundant talus (rockfall debris) indicates that rockfalls are rather frequent here on this potentially unstable slope.

Here, the road drops off the Third Valley glacial outwash terrace (31), down to the Youngest Valley terrace. This lower terrace is composed of the most recent outwash, carried downvalley by meltwater streams from a Youngest Valley glacier in the Roaring Fork, whose terminal moraine (30) borders the town of Aspen on the east.

The prominent topographic bench on Red Mountain, across the Roaring Fork Valley to the north (Plate 15B), is composed of moraine (30) of the Second Valley glaciation. The glacier that deposited this moraine extended at least as far downvalley as the Aspen airport (Sardy Field), and the moraine buried Red Butte. This bench is a remnant of the moraine, most of which has been removed by erosion. Notice the large boulders in the moraine near the west end of Red Mountain.

The horizontal scar on the hillside above the bench is an irrigation ditch, which runs through a still older moraine bench, that of the Oldest Valley glaciation.

2.15 *Bridge over the Roaring Fork River*

The Roaring Fork has cut its channel about eight feet below the surface of the Youngest Valley glacial outwash plain. A lag concentrate of rounded boulders of various rock types, derived from the outwash deposits, remains in the river bed. Flood flows have been adequate to wash away the smaller rocks and sand, leaving only the larger boulders.

2.20 *Parking lot on left for the Rio Grande Trail. See that log for site description.*

2.45 *Small pullout on right, or larger one on left a little beyond*

As we mentioned earlier, the Second Valley glacial moraine covered Red Butte. Prior to the glaciation that produced that moraine, the Roaring Fork Valley was not as deep as it is today, and Red Butte was only a low, narrow spur jutting southward from the west end of Red Mountain, with the Roaring Fork River flowing to the south of its southern end. Following the deposition of the Second Valley moraine, the Roaring Fork shifted its channel northward, so that when it began to cut down through the moraine it was situated over the Red Butte ridge. The river continued to cut down to and below its former level, slicing a narrow channel through the ridge and isolating Red Butte to the south (Plate 6B).

In looking at the sequence of sedimentary formations in Red Butte, you should recall that this sequence is now upside down, so that the oldest rocks, on the east, are above the younger ones, to the west. In that same order, the easternmost rock unit on Red Butte is the State Bridge Formation (13), originally mud and sand washed westward by rivers flowing off the broad slope that extended toward the west from the newly risen Appalachian Mountains in eastern North America about 240 million years ago. Local western sources also contributed to the State Bridge.

The soft, bright red rock that forms the north face of Red Butte, and gives it much of its color, is the Chinle Formation (14). This unit consists of lithified mud, sand, and volcanic ash, mainly derived from more local uplifts, especially in southern Arizona, where there was considerable volcanic activity, and in Nevada, where a new mountain chain was beginning to rise.

After the Chinle was deposited, beach and dune sands were laid down at the edge of the Sundance Sea, which encroached southward on the region from Canada about 162 million years ago. These sands are preserved as the Entrada Sandstone (15), the lightcolored rock immediately west of the Chinle. A prominent pinnacle of Entrada stands on this side of the river gorge, to your right (Plates 14A and 15B).

Farther downstream, beyond three intervening formations, is a dark gray rock unit called the Mancos Shale (19). This is a very thick formation, representing mud washed eastward into a later and more extensive seaway that covered the entire Rocky Mountain region from the Arctic Ocean to the Gulf of Mexico about 100 million years ago. The source of the mud was the great Western Cordillera, a high mountain chain that extended unbroken from Alaska to southern Mexico. Later on, these mountains were broken by steep faults, and they sank into the deserts of Nevada and Utah while new mountains arose in the Rocky Mountain region farther east.

Through the Roaring Fork River gorge here, a prominent ridge, covered with sagebrush, can be seen rising above the Third Valley glacial outwash plain (Plate 6B). This is a *recessional moraine* of the Second Valley glaciation, deposited when the glacier front paused there for a while during its retreat upvalley under a warming climate. The next glaciation didn't extend this far downvalley, but its outwash did, burying the lower part of this moraine. The road here is cut through moraine of the same age (Second Valley).

3.55 *Pullout on right on curve*

A better view may be had from here of the recessional moraine mentioned at the last stop, and of the younger outwash plain in which it has been partly buried (Plate 7A). At this point, the Roaring Fork River has cut its channel down about 120 feet below the surface of the glacial outwash plain. Downcutting by rivers is controlled by several factors, including the deposition of landslide debris, glacial moraine or other sediment in the valley, local or regional uplift of the land, and climatic change. All three of these have occurred fairly frequently in the Aspen area.

South of the Aspen airport (Sardy Field) is a long, low ridge. This is a *lateral moraine*, deposited at the southern edge of the same Second Valley glacier that left the recessional moraine to the east of the airport. Behind the lateral moraine is a vaguely outlined terrace of moraine from the Oldest Valley glaciation. The hilly country to the right of the lateral moraine ridge is composed of Mancos Shale (19).

The bank of the roadcut at this stop is in Second Valley moraine. Notice the wide range in size and composition of the rock fragments: clay to rounded boulders; granite, red sandstone and dark shale. This heterogeneity is characteristic of glacial moraine.

4.35 *Just beyond a curve to the left (no pullout)*

The gently sloping pasture to the right is a mudflow deposit that came from Trentaz Gulch to the east. The flat-topped, steep, brushy bluffs above this mudflow fan are glacial outwash deposits of the Oldest Valley glaciation, the first of the valley glaciations in the Roaring Fork. Younger outwash terraces are successively lower, reflecting the progressive deepening of the Roaring Fork Valley over time.

4.90 *No pullout*

The flattish surface ahead, on which the mudflow fan spreads out from Trentaz Gulch, is on glacial outwash of the Second Valley glaciation.

5.65 *W/J Ranch driveway (don't stop)*

Here, the road turns left and drops down off this outwash terrace through Grey Gulch to the terrace of the next younger (Third Valley) glaciation below. This lower terrace is the same surface on which the town of Aspen is situated. Finally, the road drops off this surface, too, onto a still lower one, that of the most recent glacial outwash (Youngest Valley) near the level of the Roaring Fork River.

6.40 *Pullout on right at bottom of hill just before an intersection*

To the right is a high roadcut in Third Valley glacial outwash. Notice how different outwash appears from moraine: while moraine has a wide range of rock fragment sizes, the water-sorted cobbles of this outwash deposit are mostly very similar in size, although the size may vary from one layer to the next. Coarser material was deposited by stronger floods.

6.75 *No pullout*

In this long roadcut (Plate 7B), outwash gravel from the Third Valley glaciation overlies a flat *strath terrace* cut on dark Mancos Shale (19). This surface was the bottom of the Roaring Fork Valley at the end of that glaciation, and the gravels were laid down upon it as the glacier melted. Since then, the Roaring Fork has cut down below that surface to its present level.

7.85 *Bridge across Woody Creek*

7.90 *Flat surface on left*

This plain is composed of glacial outwash gravel from the most recent glaciation, the Youngest Valley. The Roaring Fork has cut its channel only a few feet below this surface. The next higher outwash plain, of the next older glaciation (Third Valley), is on the right, just above the tracks of the Denver & Rio Grande Western Railroad.

8.50 *Pull off left into a gravel frontage road just before the railroad crossing*

Looking east from here, you can see all four glacial outwash surfaces. You're standing on the Youngest Valley outwash, the lowest. The next older, and higher, the Third Valley, is to your left, across the road. Above that, very prominent, and extending far to the south, is the next older, the Second Valley. The Oldest Valley surface is above that, also very prominent. Red Mountain, capped by Ice Cap glacial moraine, rises above the highest surface. Across the valley, the prominent terrace, with Colorado State Highway 82 running along it, is composed of Third Valley outwash. The town of Aspen sits on this same surface, as we mentioned previously.

10.00 *Fork in the road; stay right; pull out at the base of a steep slope on the right*

The black, rounded boulders covering this slope are basalt derived from a lava flow near the top of the slope, 1200 feet above you. This flow was erupted 1.5 million years ago on a former, broad valley floor of the Roaring Fork River. Since then, the present river valley has been cut down 1200 feet, almost a foot per 1000 years. The flow is centered on the Castle Creek fault zone, mentioned earlier in this log. Probably little movement occurred along the Castle Creek fault 1.5 million years ago, because remnants of the old Roaring Fork Valley floor surface have not been significantly dropped to the west of the fault below their counterparts to the east; but broad, regional uplift probably occurred at that time, which would have induced mountain glaciation and initiated downcutting by the Roaring Fork River.

Lincoln Creek Road

¼ day, 6¼ miles; elevation gain about 752 feet from Colorado State Highway 82, at 9785 feet to Grizzly Reservoir outlet at 10,537 feet.

USGS Topographic Quadrangle Maps: New York Peak and Independence Pass.

Access: Start at mile 10.80 of the Independence Pass Road. Lincoln Creek Road takes off to the right. The road is ungraded dirt, but passable for most cars if driven slowly and carefully.

0.00 *Roadhead*

The bedrock here is biotite gneiss (1) near its contact with quartz monzonite (3) to the south. The biotite gneiss was originally deposited as mud and dirty sand, probably in a deep, offshore basin, about 1.9 billion years ago. It is the oldest rock in the Aspen district. These sediments in time became consolidated into shale and graywacke. Between 1.7 and 1.45 billion years ago, they were metamorphosed to gneiss during the intrusion of granodiorite (2) and quartz monzonite (3), both granitic igneous rock units.

The unconsolidated earth material overlying the bedrock here in places is Youngest Valley glacial moraine (30), contrasting with the biotite gneiss in being one of the youngest geological units in the district. Its diverse mixture of clay, silt, sand, pebbles and rounded cobbles and boulders of various rock types was laid down by the most recent of several glaciers that flowed down the Roaring Fork Valley. Since this glacier melted, the Roaring Fork River has reestablished itself, and has cut a shallow channel here beneath the surface of the glacial moraine. In some places, where the moraine is thicker, the channel cut is much deeper.

1.45 Hummocky ground

Surfaces covered by glacial moraine are characteristically hummocky, especially if the moraine is fairly recent and unmodified by erosion.

1.75 Pullout on right

This spectacularly sculptured rocky gorge was carved by Lincoln Creek through a bedrock irregularity in the floor of the valley. This situation may arise in either or both of two ways. A glacier moving downvalley destroys the original gradient profile of the valley that was created by the stream. Where the rock of the valley floor is resistant, the glacier will erode it less, but where it's weak, the glacier will readily excavate the bedrock floor. This causes a stairstep, or "tread and riser" profile to develop in the valley floor. When the stream becomes reestablished after the glacier melts, it will then cut deep, narrow channels through the "stairs" in order to restore its former smooth gradient.

The other possibility is that the stream may have changed its course since the glaciation. Glaciers leave fairly thick, irregular deposits of moraine in their valleys, and when the stream reestablishes itself, usually it begins by flowing on moraine. The stream will automatically choose that path which is closest to a smooth profile, and this is inevitably a different path from the one it followed before the deposition of the moraine, because the path is determined by the configuration of the moraine surface.

The stream will then continue to cut down through the moraine as it attempts to find the best gradient possible for its rate of flow and its sediment load. In the process, it usually encounters various bedrock ridges that used to be located some distance away from the stream before the glaciation. Sawing down through these ridges is a great deal easier than moving the channel to softer ground, and so bedrock gorges are formed. Probably most such gorges were formed by a combination of these two processes.

Toward the west end of the gorge, the rock type changes from black and pinkish-gray biotite gneiss (1) to light gray quartz monzonite (3). This, then, is the edge of one of the large, granitic intrusive bodies that metamorphosed the gneiss about 1½ billion years ago. The change in rock type is probably an important factor in the presence of the bedrock ridge at this point, since the biotite gneiss appears to be somewhat more resistant to erosion than the quartz monzonite.

1.95 *First large clearing*

Most subalpine meadows, like this one, have violent origins. The steep mountain slopes to the north and south generate snow avalanches, which plunge with great force down the chutes visible on these slopes, snapping off any trees that may be growing in their paths. Several such broken trees may be seen in this meadow. Low growing plants, like bog birch and Pacific willow, are able to survive in avalanche paths, as they do here, along with young aspens.

2.10 *Pullout on right by bedrock exposure*

This is another small gorge cut by Lincoln Creek through a bedrock irregularity. This one has a stone arch cut in the biotite gneiss. To the left of the road, the glacially polished bedrock surface is incised by a large, shallow groove formed by boulders embedded in the base of the moving glacier.

2.60 *Old rockslide on left*

The age of this slide is indicated by the mature growth of lichen and aspen on and among the boulders. A more recent slide would have less vegetation growing on it.

2.75 *Large boulder on left*

Sizeable rocks like this one are easily moved by glaciers and are often left perched in rather improbable places. The beautiful, contorted banding in this boulder is typical of a variety of gneiss called *migmatite*, in which magma has been injected between the foliation planes of the rock under high pressure (Plate 8A).

3.05 *Just west of a small campground*

Cutting an outcrop of biotite gneiss on the left side of the road is a vein of pegmatite, a coarse-grained variety of granite, whose unusually large crystals of glassy quartz, clear, platy muscovite, chalky feldspar and black, platy biotite grew to such sizes with the assistance of a high percentage of water in the magma.

Beyond the campground, and also on the left, is a low, glacially scoured outcrop, most of which consists of a large dike of porphyritic granodiorite. The dike was injected into the surrounding country rock about 34 million years ago at about the same time that the formidable Grizzly caldera underwent a series of catastrophic volcanic explosions a few miles to the southeast.

3.25 *Bog on right, just west of New York Creek Trail*

Lakes and ponds are temporary phenomena in Nature. Where one exists, something has happened to block the normal flow of a stream toward the ocean. Here, the recent disruption caused by mountain glaciation is responsible. But this former pond has nearly been obliterated by silt carried downvalley by Lincoln Creek. Perhaps the best example of glacially disrupted drainage in North America is the state of Minnesota, the "Land of 10,000 Lakes."

Across the bog on the mountainside to the south is a large avalanche chute. Snow avalanches begin in the broad bowl below the peak and sweep down the chute, clearing it of any young trees that may have grown there since the previous avalanche. Rock debris also slides down the same chute, and accumulates in the symmetrical *talus cone* at its base.

This peak is composed entirely of volcanic ash (24). When the Grizzly caldera exploded, many cubic miles of magma were blown into the atmosphere in an atomized state. This enormous cloud of magma retained most of its heat as it rose, and it must have illuminated the surrounding countryside for hundreds of miles. As the molten magmatic ash settled to the ground, it fused into a solid mass known as *welded tuff*. Much of the countryside southeast of Aspen is composed of this deposit.

3.55 *Meadow*

This is another subalpine clearing caused and maintained by snow avalanches.

Notice the different appearance of the mountains ahead compared with those behind you. To the east, the steeper, less vegetated slopes of 34-million-year-old intrusive porphyries (22) and welded tuffs (24) show more talus (rockslide debris) and rockslide gullies in contrast with the gentler but more rugged, and better vegetated slopes of biotite gneiss to the west. From here on, you will be driving within the Grizzly caldera. This formidable explosion vent measures about nine miles in diameter.

3.90 *Road crosses a small stream*

3.95 *Outcrop on left*

This is a granodiorite porphyry intrusive (22) related to the development of the Grizzly caldera. The finer grain of the groundmass, or matrix, indicates that this rock cooled more quickly than did the porphyritic granodiorite dike at mile 3.05. Notice the larger crystals (phenocrysts) of feldspar and biotite.

4.45 *Recent rockslide on right*

A hazard to be considered when constructing a road across a steep slope is evident here. Notice the lack of vegetation on the slide.

4.90 *Ponds on right*

These are beaver ponds. An old, overgrown lodge is visible on the far side of the closest pond. Since the beavers' favorite dam construction materials, aspen and narrowleaf poplar, are unavailable here, these particular dams are made chiefly of mud.

Between the road and the ponds is a large, amphitheater-like spring bowl. Water seeping out of the hillside at this point serves to accelerate erosion by flushing away the weathered rock and soil material as fast as it forms. The principal weathering processes here are freezing, thawing, and oxidation of the underlying bedrock.

5.00 *Road crosses a gully*

This gully has been cut by stream floods within an avalanche chute.

5.25 *Meadow below avalanche chute on left*

Where Lincoln Creek makes a broad right turn, it has eroded a steep cutbank in the valley slope, while a gentle "slip-off" slope has formed within the bend.

5.45 *Meadow below avalanche chute on left*

The hummocky ridge to the right of the road is probably the toe of a landslide, although it might also be glacial moraine. Hummocky topography, present here on both sides of the road, is characteristic of both moraine and landslide deposits. Distinguishing one from the other is often difficult, especially where the landslide material is derived from moraine, as here.

6.25 *Outlet of the artificial Grizzly Reservoir. From here, continue uphill on the left fork of the road, ahead. After a short distance, the road descends again into Portal Campground. The trailhead for the Grizzly Lake Trail is at the top of the rise between here and the campground.*

Maroon Creek Road

¼ day, 9½ miles; elevation gain 1691 feet from Aspen, at 7909 feet to Maroon Lake Campground at 9600 feet.

USGS Topographic Quadrangle Maps: Aspen, Highland Peak and Maroon Bells.

USGS Geologic Quadrangle Maps: Aspen GQ-933, Highland Peak GQ-932, and Maroon Bells GQ-788.

Access: From the Jerome Hotel, Main and Mill streets, Aspen, drive 1.3 miles west on Main Street (Colorado State Highway 82) to the intersection with Maroon Creek and Castle Creek roads by the Aspen Chapel, a large, modern, stone church. Turn left off Highway 82 and take the right hand road.

0.00 *For a description of the roadhead, see the Castle Creek log*

1.10 *Pullout on right by a wooden fence*

The cutbank ahead on the left is typical glacial moraine (30) of the Third Valley glaciation. Notice the unstratified and heterogeneous mixture of rock types and sizes from clay to rounded boulders.

1.20 *Pullout on right opposite end of wooden fence on left*

This deep gorge has been cut by Maroon Creek since the deposition of the moraine of the Third Valley glaciation. Probably, Maroon Creek originally flowed somewhat farther east than it does today. The flow of the creek was shut off while the valley was glaciated. When it began to run again, after the melting of the glacier, the creek was directed westward to the low topographic line between the moraine and the bedrock slope to the west. When the creek cut downward to reach its former level, it was forced to cut its channel through bedrock.

The alternating greenish claystone and limestone beds exposed here in the gorge belong to the Morrison Formation (16), whose deposition, about 151 to 140 million years ago, resulted from the uplift of the Western Cordillera, a high mountain range extending from Alaska through Nevada. Mud, sand and volcanic ash were washed and blown eastward from the Cordillera and deposited on an extensive river floodplain that existed then on the site of the present Rocky Mountain region before the uplift of the modern Rockies and after the wearing-down of the Ancestral Rocky Mountains. Now, these originally flat-lying sediments are dipping northward at about a 20-degree angle.

Two geological events were principally responsible for the tilting. The first was the uplift of the Sawatch Range to the east of Castle Creek about 70 million years ago. As we mentioned in the roadhead description for the Castle Creek road log, the thick sedimentary cover that overlay the west flank of the Sawatch Range broke loose and slid westward on the soft Belden Formation (9) during the uplift. This colossal *gravity glide sheet* now forms the Elk Mountains southwest of Aspen.

The second geological event was the intrusion of granodiorite magma (22) into the basal glide plane beneath the glide sheet. This domed up the Elk Mountains, producing most of the northward tilt we see here today.

Above the gorge, a steep slope, covered with oak brush, is able to withstand erosion because of its composition: dense moraine of the Third Valley glaciation.

1.60 *Driveway on right; cutbank ahead on left*

The material in this roadcut differs from glacial moraine in being crudely stratified and in having a narrower range of rock particle sizes (Plate 8B). Deposits of this sort, called *kame terraces,* form at the sides of a melting glacier where meltwater flushes moraine material off the glacier surface. Finer sand and mud are washed away while large boulders are too big to be moved by the flowing water. Only a limited range of particle sizes is moved to the glacier margin and deposited there between the ice and the bedrock wall of the valley.

Notice how the roots of shrubs and trees growing at the top of the roadcut serve to protect the cut from further erosion.

1.90 *Bridge across Maroon Creek*

2.10 *Large, high cutbank on right*

This, again, is a kame terrace, probably originally connected with the one farther downstream before Maroon Creek cut its present channel.

2.20 *Pullout on left; cutbank on right*

This is Third Valley glacial moraine (30). It contains unstratified, heterogeneous rock types and rock particle sizes, and rounded boulders.

2.45 *Horse pasture on right*

The gently rolling surface of this pasture is the top of the Third Valley glacial moraine.

2.95 *Flat land by Maroon Creek*

Left to itself, and undisturbed, a stream will tend to carve its channel into a smoothly graded curve concave toward the sky, the steepness and concavity of the curve determined essentially by the requirement of moving water and erosional rock waste off the land as fast as they accumulate. Steeper gradients are required where streamflow is less, because gravity is more effective on steeper slopes. For the same reason, concavity is greater where streamflow (volume of water flowing per unit of time) increases downstream.

Glaciers disturb this ideal geometry by irregularly eroding the bedrock floors of valleys and by depositing moraine. When a stream becomes reestablished after a glacier melts, it will cut down through humps and fill hollows with gravel, sand and mud until it once again has a semblance of its ideal, graded curve. This alluvial floodplain (33) is an example of a filled hollow.

3.50 *Gentle, aspen-covered slope ahead*

Rockfall debris (32) forms this gently sloping, fan-shaped surface. Aspens often cover these rocky deposits until sufficient soil accumulates to support coniferous trees.

3.90 *Pullout on left; Maroon Creek trailhead*

Across the creek and a bit downstream is a fresh, unvegetated, linear landslide scar. A second slide scar is opposite the Maroon Creek trailhead. This one also has an unvegetated, linear channel which curves to the right as it descends a vegetated cone of talus (rockslide debris) at the base.

4.65 *Pullout on left*

A large mudflow came out of the gully across Maroon Creek and dammed the valley until the creek cut a new channel through the toe of the mudflow. Back down the road a short distance, on the west side of the valley, you will notice a large stand of aspen poplar in which the trees have been broken or bent over uphill. This was the work of a large snow avalanche that came down the same gully as the mudflow and rushed up the opposite slope. Such major avalanches don't occur very frequently, as is evident from the age of the aspens.

5.05 *Entrance to Maroon Creek Campground*

The red rock that forms the valley walls here is Maroon Formation (12), an assemblage of shale, sandstone, limestone, and conglomerate representing weathered rock and soil washed southwestward from the Ancestral Front Range, 290 million years ago. This range rose to heights probably exceeding 10,000 feet a little west of the position of the present Front Range. The Maroon Formation is a little more than three miles thick here!

In the glaciated valley of Maroon Creek, the rather soft bedrock valley walls have been oversteepened beyond their normal slope angle by glacial erosion. Rockslides are gradually working to reestablish the normal, gentler slope angle of the valley walls.

5.35 *Pullout on left; U-shaped valley on left skyline*

This is a hanging glacial valley (Plate 9A). The large glacier in the Maroon Creek Valley eroded the bedrock much more than the smaller glacier in this tributary valley did. Consequently, the tributary now enters the Maroon Creek Valley 1200 feet up on its eastern slope. Youngest Valley moraine (30) is present on the floor of the hanging valley.

5.80 *Cutbank on right*

Landslide deposits, such as this one, composed of red silt and rock debris from the Maroon Formation, are usually distinguished from glacial moraine by the angularity of their rock fragments.

6.80 *Pullout on left; park and walk back about 100 feet*

Across the creek is a large avalanche chute with a mudflow alluvial fan at its base (Plate 9B). At the sides of the avalanche path on the fan, mature stands of aspen indicate the limits of large snow avalanches. A younger stand on the left side of the path has grown since the last major avalanche, but smaller slides have destroyed it in the central part of the path where only herbaceous vegetation is growing at present.

As you drive on from here, notice the large avalanche bowl on the left skyline with multiple avalanche chutes descending its slopes (Plate 10A).

7.60 *Pullout on left before cattle guard*

From here, you can see the 14,000-foot peaks of the Maroon Bells up Maroon Creek canyon to the right (Plate 10B). These mountains are composed of Maroon Formation, dipping about 20 degrees to the north. They owe most of their high elevation and erosion resistance to the presence beneath them of the White Rock Granodiorite (22), which intruded the Elk Mountain area about 34 million years ago. As we mentioned earlier, the rocks of the Elk Range slid westward off the rising Sawatch Range about 72 million years ago under the influence of gravity. Pyramid

Peak, another 14,000+-foot peak, is visible here to the east of the Maroon Bells.

The prominent hill straight ahead, separating two valleys, is a *medial glacial moraine* of the Youngest Valley glaciation. Rock debris from two confluent glaciers accumulated here on the divide between the two valleys. Scattered, fallen, dead tree trunks on the east face indicate a major fire. Aspen has revegetated the lower slopes.

Across the road is a V-shaped gully formed by landslides and used also by snow avalanches in winter. The road cuts across the top of the landslide debris fan at the base of the gully. Notice the lack of trees and shrubs in the gully and the bent young aspens below the road.

9.50 *Maroon Lake Campground parking lot; Buckskin Pass trailhead. For site description, see that trail log.*

Trail Logs

Ute Trail

½ day, 1 mile; elevation gain 1500 feet from the trailhead at 8000 feet to Ute Lookout at 9500 feet.

USGS Topographic Quadrangle Map: Aspen
USGS Geologic Quadrangle Map: Aspen GQ-933.

Access: From the Jerome Hotel, follow Main Street (Colorado State Highway 82) 0.25 mile east, then 0.30 mile south to where it intersects Ute Avenue just beyond a wood-fenced lawn with ponds on the left. Go 0.40 mile east on Ute Avenue to where the pavement ends by a medium-sized parking lot on the left with a sign saying Ute Park. A private drive angles back uphill on the right. Just beyond this drive is the trailhead, marked by three steps made from old railroad ties.

Stop 1: *Trailhead in an aspen grove*

The front of the Third Valley glacier in the Roaring Fork stopped here, at the east edge of Aspen (Plate 12B). Glaciers continue to advance downvalley only as long as their rate of flow remains higher than their rate of melting. Flow increases when snow accumulates more rapidly on the higher portions of the glacier; melting increases with a rise in average summer temperature. When the rate of melting equals the rate of flow, the glacier stops advancing, and its front stays in one place in the valley while the flow of the ice continues to bring rock debris downvalley to be dumped in a hummocky deposit of clay, silt, sand, gravel, and rounded cobbles and boulders, known as a *terminal moraine* (30).

To the west, the flat land on which the town of Aspen is situated is *glacial outwash* (31) consisting of cobbles, gravel, and sand washed down from the glacier by floods of melting icewater.

From here, the trail ascends the steep northeast spur of Ajax, or Aspen Mountain, by a series of nineteen switchbacks. (Note: be sure to keep track of the number of switchbacks on the trail, since the various stops are referred to by switchback number. A switchback is a straight section of trail between two sharp bends that reverse the trail direction, Plate 11A.)

Stop 2: *Clearing just beyond trailhead*

This meadow is the bottom of both a rockslide path and a snow avalanche path. If it were not for the frequent occurrence of relatively small snow avalanches in winter, this spot would be nearly as densely forested as the surrounding slopes. Notice the angular rock fragments lying on the ground. These are characteristic of rockslide deposits (32), and help to distinguish such deposits from similar-appearing glacial moraine (30).

Just above the west end of the first switchback on the trail is a Douglas-fir with an S-shaped trunk and a long, vertical scar on the uphill side. This is a snow avalanche victim. Unusually vigorous growth on the underside of a leaning tree will cause the trunk to grow upward again, thereby righting the tree. Usually, as here, the trunk will overshoot the vertical, whereupon vigorous growth begins on the other side. Eventually, vertical growth is resumed above the bent portion of the trunk. Watch for more such "avalanche trees" as you go on.

Stop 3: *West end of fifth switchback; edge of avalanche path*

The dead Douglas-fir here has been knocked down by at least two separate avalanches, as may be seen by its contorted growth form. Recall the "avalanche tree" you saw lower down, and see if you can visualize the sequence of events that produced the contortions in this tree.

Stop 4: *Middle of seventh switchback*

Here is another avalanche tree, again a Douglas-fir.

Stop 5: *Eighth switchback (very long)*

Vegetation types indicate the nature and intensity of some geologic processes. This switchback crosses frequently active ava-

1A. Ajax, or Aspen Mountain, once yielded a fortune in silver; now its famous ski runs yield a more lasting fortune in recreation. The town of Aspen rests on a plain of glacial outwash gravel at the foot of the mountain.

1B. Aspen's fall rainbow, Red Mountain wears aspen golds and greens over bright red shales of the 290-million-year-old Maroon Formation.

2A. The Roaring Fork belies its name in this quiet stretch east of Aspen, where it meanders peacefully across a gently sloping floodplain behind a natural dam of Third Valley glacial moraine.

2B. Jagged blocks of granite at the base of a steep cliff bespeak a major rockfall near Weller Campground. Engelmann spruce and subalpine fir find a favorable habitat for growth in this rocky ground.

3A. Smoothed bedrock and perched boulders give evidence of glaciation in the Roaring Fork Valley near the old Grottos Campground.

3B. Glacial scouring of granitic bedrock produces distinctive forms, like this "whaleback" ridge.

4A. Rushing floodwaters have carved a narrow, tortuous flume through the glacially smoothed granitic outcrop. Ice often persists through the summer in the cold, shady micro-environment at the bottom of the flume.

4B. Snow avalanches from the upper slopes of Green Mountain keep this chute and the rock debris fan below it free of spruce and fir forest. The mountain is composed of 1.47-billion-year-old quartz monzonite.

5A. Rivers carve their own valleys, but here, below Independence Pass, the youthful Roaring Fork has had assistance from valley glaciers, which deepened the stream valley and scoured it into a U-shape.

5B. Castle and Maroon creeks have carved the long, high ridge of Highland Peak from the Elk Mountain uplift, southwest of Aspen. The Maroon Bells, on the crest of the uplift, appear in the notch between Highland and Sievers peaks.

6A. The broad, level summit plateau of Smuggler Mountain, dark with a subalpine forest of spruce and fir, is an old land surface, once continuous with the Great Plains. Aspen and oak cover Smuggler's lower slopes.

6B. Through the Roaring Fork gorge at Red Butte, the recessional moraine ridge of the Second Valley glacier is visible, partly buried in Third Valley glacial outwash gravel. Montane brush grows in the foreground.

7A. Another view of the Second Valley recessional moraine, and the Roaring Fork gorge, cut about 120 feet below the Third Valley outwash gravel plain. Ski trails on Highland Peak and Buttermilk Mountain are visible in the background.

7B. Between two glaciations, the Roaring Fork cut its valley down to the level top of this Mancos Shale outcrop. Outwash gravel from the Third Valley glacier then covered the valley bottom. Finally, the river cut down through both outwash and bedrock to its present level.

8A. Migmatite is a spectacular hybrid rock: originally a banded gneiss into which igneous magma has been injected between the foliation planes. This outcrop in the bed of Lincoln Creek has been scoured by flowing water and sand.

8B. The crudely stratified deposits of a kame terrace in the Maroon Creek Valley preserve gravels that were laid down by meltwater between a stagnant glacier and the valley wall.

9A. Glacial moraine, extending downslope from the hanging glacial valley above Maroon Creek, supports a stand of aspen poplar where moisture drains from the cirque above.

9B. A large snow avalanche cleared this alluvial fan up to the mature aspens on the far left. Since then, a smaller avalanche cleared the younger growth except for a narrow strip parallel with the edge of the earlier clearing. Strata of 280-million-year-old Maroon siltstone dip gently northward off the Elk Range uplift.

10A. The source of the avalanches mentioned in the previous figure. Several steep chutes feed the main channel below the avalanche bowl.

10B. The base of the large hill in the foreground is sheathed in aspen-covered medial moraine, deposited at the junction of two glaciers. Pyramid Peak rises beyond the hill. The Maroon Bells are to the right.

11A. Snow avalanche paths through a forest of Douglas-fir mark the steep north slope of Ajax, or Aspen Mountain, where the Ute Trail ascends by nineteen switchbacks to a spectacular lookout high above Aspen.

11B. White bands of flint in gray dolomite lend the Manitou Formation a striking appearance. Here, an outcrop on the forest floor is flanked by maple and serviceberry shrubs.

12A. The overturned fault block of Red Butte dominates the glacial outwash plain northwest of Aspen. The gorge of the Roaring Fork winds beyond Red Butte toward Basalt Mountain and the distant White River Plateau. Most of the country to the west of Aspen is part of an enormous slice of sedimentary rock that slid westward off the rising Sawatch Range about 70 million years ago.

12B. The bouldery channel of the Roaring Fork and hummocky terrain overgrown with aspens outline the terminal deposits of a Third Valley glacier that stopped at the east edge of Aspen.

13A. High-level benches and a hanging glacial valley on Smuggler Mountain mark the heights to which former glaciers filled the Roaring Fork Valley, now floored by a nearly level floodplain. This valley has been cut over 2000 feet down by stream and glacial erosion within the past 1.5 million years.

13B. A meander bend in the Roaring Fork marks a small alluvial pocket in the Third Valley terminal moraine just east of Aspen. Blue spruce and aspen poplar grow in the valley. The foreground trees are Douglas-fir.

14A. A gallery of narrowleaf poplar, or cottonwood, flanks the Roaring Fork along its course through the Red Butte gorge. Glacial boulders stud the river channel, and a pinnacle of Entrada Sandstone pierces the western skyline.

14B. Ripplemarks, produced by wave action in shallow water above a muddy sea floor, are preserved in this mudstone boulder.

15A. The first product of a new geological regime in North America, the varicolored sandy shales of the Morrison Formation were derived from the uplift of the great Western Cordillera in Nevada about 150 million years ago.

15B. Giant boulders of Entrada Sandstone block the old railroad bed below the crag from which they fell in recent years. Note the fresh scar in the upper left. In the right center, below the aspen-covered slopes of Red Mountain, is a bouldery terrace of Second Valley glacial moraine.

16A. A wildly twisted blue spruce (left) clings to an unstable perch on a steep slope of interlayered shale and limestone of the Mancos Shale. A drag fold in limestone (upper right) indicates uplift toward the right.

16B. Glacial moraine is a heterogeneous mixture of rounded boulders and cobbles, gravel, sand, silt and clay torn from diverse rock formations by glaciers and transported up to hundreds of miles.

17A. The U-shaped glacial valley of Maroon Creek, its floor blazing with autumn aspen, frames the snow-dusted peaks of the Maroon Bells.

17B. Glacial erosion oversteepened this valley wall above Maroon Lake. Stream erosion is now working to reestablish a gentler slope by removing rock material from the gullies, above, and redepositing it in an alluvial fan, below.

18A. "Crater Lake," above Maroon Lake, is not a volcanic crater. It was formed when a large rockfall dammed the valley of West Maroon Creek. Spruce, fir, willow, and aspen surround the lakeshore.

18B. Effects of glaciation are evident everywhere in the Rocky Mountain highlands. Here, glacial cirques, horns, and aretes on Pyramid Peak rise above the U-shaped West Maroon Creek Valley. The trail passes through hummocky glacial ground moraine.

19A. North Maroon Peak (left) and an unnamed 13,400-foot peak rise above an alp—a high altitude meadow—below Buckskin Pass. Talus cones are abundant at the base of slopes of the easily eroded Maroon Formation.

19B. A sill of gray-green porphyritic granodiorite contrasts with red siltstone on this hillslope below Buckskin Pass. Yellow Western Paintbrush are growing in profusion amid the rock debris.

20A. Inch-long phenocrysts of pink orthoclase feldspar lend a striking appearance to this intrusive granodiorite.

20B. A persistent snow cornice endures the brief summer heat on Buckskin Pass, at 12,462-foot elevation. Frost-shattered porphyritic granodiorite lies to the left of the cornice, Maroon siltstone to the right.

21A. Close cousins to ice glaciers, rock glaciers like this one just west of Buckskin Pass are moved by the same mechanism: the slow flow of ice within the glacier.

21B. High benches above glaciated valleys are known as alps. Above this alp on the Roaring Fork, the skyline ridge is cut on an old land surface that once extended from the Colorado Plateau eastward to the Great Plains.

22A. The headwaters of the Roaring Fork River spring within Independence Lake, a glacial tarn at 12,600 feet elevation.

22B. Beyond Independence Lake, a large rock glacier, flowing off the northwest shoulder of Blue Mountain, is encroaching upon a small companion lake to Independence. Grizzly Peak dominates the right skyline.

23A. Frost polygons on an alpine pass provide an illustration of how the annual freezing and thawing of water within soil above permanently frozen ground can sort and move rock and soil material.

23B. Layering parallel to the hillslope in Second Valley glacial moraine on Smuggler Mountain facilitated this major landslide, which dumped thousands of tons of bouldery gravel into Hunter Creek.

24A. September snow caps the peaks of the Elk Range. This level meadow in the Hunter Creek Valley is floored by bouldery moraine of the Third Valley glaciation.

24B. Flanked by Smuggler Mountain on the left and Red Mountain on the right, the Hunter Creek Valley plunges abruptly into the valley of the Roaring Fork opposite the broad dome of the Elk Range. The Maroon Bells are on the far left, Mount Daly on the far right.

lanche paths with scant vegetation except for a few annual herbs, less active paths with various shrubs and young aspens, and areas of infrequent or no avalanching with mature Douglas-fir forest.

At the east end of the switchback is an outcrop of quartz monzonite (3). This 1.47-billion-year-old granitic rock is composed of pinkish potassium feldspar, greasy-gray quartz, dark, flaky biotite mica, and light, flaky muscovite mica. Decomposition of biotite and perhaps other iron-bearing minerals sparingly present has produced a rusty film of limonite on the surface of the outcrop.

Three intersecting sets of parallel *joints*, or fractures, cut this outcrop, reflecting major forces that have twisted, bent and broken the rocks of the Aspen district. By studying the orientations of large numbers of such joint sets, geologists can reconstruct the stress fields that acted upon the rocks in which they occur. In general, the stresses that produced the Rocky Mountain ranges about 70 million years ago were *compressional* and *right-lateral,* which means that the major fracture systems, oriented mainly north-northwesterly, had their eastern sides moving south and their western sides north. The plate tectonic explanation for this pattern of fracturing is given under *The Geologic Setting.*

The quartz monzonite is exceeded in age only by two other rock units: a 1.7-billion-year-old granodiorite (2) in the Independence Pass region, and the widespread biotite gneiss (1) of the Sawatch Range, into which both the quartz monzonite and the granodiorite were intruded as igneous magma in a liquid state.

Stop 6: *West end of the ninth switchback*

This switchback ends just short of a large snow avalanche chute, bare of vegetation, whose path is floored by mineral soil and rock fragments.

Most of the Douglas-firs on this switchback have scars on their uphill sides, indicating the rather frequent occurrence of rockfalls on this slope. In the bend of the switchback is a young Douglas-fir that has been bent over by an avalanche or rockfall, and what was formerly a branch near the base has assumed vertical growth as a new trunk.

The tenth switchback is very short.

Stop 7: *Seventeenth switchback*

The angular, pinkish-white rock fragments strewn about the slope here are from the Sawatch Quartzite (4), the first of a sequence of sedimentary formations deposited upon the much older quartz monzonite. The Sawatch Quartzite began its existence as a white quartz beach sand deposited at the shoreline of a shallow sea that advanced eastward across the western United States about half a billion years ago. This and overlying rock layers, originally roughly horizontal, have been tilted upward at steep angles during the uplift of the Sawatch mountain range, of which Aspen Mountain is the westernmost peak. The uplift has proceeded intermittently since about 72 million years ago.

The eighteenth switchback is very short.

Stop 8: *About 100 feet along the nineteenth switchback*

Above the trail is an outcrop of Sawatch Quartzite in which the strata (rock layers) are dipping at about 40 degrees to the northwest.

Stop 9: *Farther along the ninteenth switchback*

Largely hidden by the rosy-buff-colored soil is the Peerless Formation (5), a mixture of quartz sandstone, dolomite, and a little shale. This rock unit was deposited as sand and limy mud on top of the Sawatch Quartzite after the shoreline had moved some distance eastward, and the Aspen area was under a moderate depth of water. Occasional pieces of the Peerless may be found amid the dirt.

Stop 10: *End of the nineteenth switchback below a rocky ridge*

The strikingly banded rock here is the Manitou Dolomite (6) which was originally laid down in a shallow, quiet sea as carbonate mud deposited from seawater. The irregular, parallel bands in the rock are layers of chert, or flint, composed of pure silicon dioxide. The origin of such layers is obscure, but their silica may have been derived from the decomposition of silicate minerals, or from the solution and reprecipitation, along bedding planes in the limestone, of other siliceous material including skeletons of sponges, which may have been abundant in the limy mud. Both the chert and the dolomite are gray on fresh exposures, but their weathered surfaces are white and buff, respectively. The Manitou Dolomite overlies the Peerless Formation, which, in turn, overlies the Sawatch Quartzite. Mountain building forces have tilted these and overlying sedimentary rock units upward to about a 50-degree angle (Plate 11B).

Stop 11: *Ute Lookout at the north end of the rocky ridge of Manitou Dolomite*

In addition to the bedding, or stratification planes, the dolomite outcrop has three intersecting sets of parallel joints which, as with those in the underlying quartz monzonite, are reflections of the ongoing forces which have disturbed this region of the Earth's crust since about 72 million years ago. The prominent flat rock surface below the iron pipe that marks the lookout is a bedding plane, forming a dip slope of 50 degrees northwest.

The forested ridge to the south is composed of the resistant Sawatch Quartzite. Paralleling this toward the west on the other side of Spar Gulch is another high ridge. At the very base of this, the Manitou Dolomite is exposed. Overlying the Manitou are the two units of the roughly 350-million-year-old Chaffee Formation (7): the lower Parting Member and the upper Dyer Dolomite. The Parting Member is a light tan sandstone and varicolored shale, originally laid down as sand and mud carried by rivers westward from the slowly emerging Ancestral Front Range to the east. The Dyer Dolomite was originally a limy mud laid down in a shallow sea that covered the Aspen area after the first pulse of uplift to the east was over.

Capping the ridge is the Leadville Limestone (8), about 340 million years old. The Gilman Sandstone Member at the base of the Leadville records a second pulse of uplift in the Ancestral Front Range. Again, the overlying carbonate (limestone and dolomite) reflects limy mud deposition from a shallow sea. Several mine tunnels, or adits, are visible along the Leadville Limestone outcrop, with mine dumps on the steep slope beneath them. Prospectors were looking for silver and lead ore mainly in the contact between the lower, dolomitic part of the Leadville and the overlying limestone. Ore was deposited there, and in other favorable stratigraphic horizons, during strong pulses of mountain building about 70 million and 34 million years ago.

This west wall of Spar Gulch is the truncated eastern limb of a major syncline, whose axis plunges due north under the town of Aspen. The youngest rocks in this great troughlike fold are the dark carbonates and oil shales of the 305-million-year-old Belden Formation (9), and a grayish to greenish porphyritic aplite (21) that intruded the Belden about 72 million years ago during the first pulse of uplift in the modern Rocky Mountains. The Belden itself is the sedimentary evidence of another much older, major uplift in the Ancestral Front Range to the east about 313 million years ago. Lime and mud, washed westward from that uplift by streams, accumulated in a poorly oxygenated, shallow basin in the Aspen area where the incomplete decomposition of dead plant and animal matter produced the oil that blackens this formation. Miners explored the Belden quite thoroughly, since ore deposition favored certain stratigraphic horizons within it. Some of the richest silver and lead deposits of the Aspen district have been mined from this formation.

Although a great thickness of sediments younger than the Belden was once present here, this was rather suddenly removed during the uplift of the Sawatch Range 72 million years ago. A sheet of rock about 20 by 50 miles in area and up to five miles thick broke loose and slid westward off the steep western flank of the Sawatch uplift here at Aspen. The soft shale of the Belden Formation served as a lubricating layer for this enormous "landslide," the rocks of which now form the Elk Range, whose peaks are among Colorado's highest. The gravity glide plane itself, known as the Elk Range thrust fault, probably lies between the ridge that tops the west wall of Spar Gulch and the next ridge west (which is composed of the aplite porphyry intrusive rock) in a small valley called Vallejo Gulch. This is floored by the soft Belden sediments, which have, on occasion, been sufficiently lubricated by groundwater to slide as mudflows down the gulch toward Aspen. Notice the fan-shaped deposit at the lower end of the gulch. This unstable history has not deterred the Aspen Ski Corporation from building a ski lift up the full length of the fan. More vulnerable than the lift are the various buildings on the downhill edge of the fan.

The far west skyline ridge of Aspen (or Ajax) Mountain is aplite on its southern end and quartz monzonite on its northern end with a small capping of sedimentary rocks including the Sawatch, the Leadville, and intervening formations on the extreme north slope of the ridge. You may recall having seen the quartz monzonite (3) on your way up the trail. Its reappearance on the west ridge of Ajax beyond the central syncline shows that, basically, Ajax is a huge, uplifted block of quartz monzonite with only a thin cover of younger sedimentary rocks on top of it.

Beyond the west ridge, the flattish cone of Mt. Sopris rises in the distance. This is one member of a series of granodiorite intrusives that accompanied the second major pulse of mountain building in the modern Rockies between 38 and 26 million years ago. Sopris is not a volcano, but it very likely had a large volcano sitting on top of it at one time. Subsequent erosion would have removed both the volcanic peak and the soft sediments overlying and surrounding the Sopris granodiorite, which was left as a prominent mountain peak due to its relatively high resistance to erosion.

The rolling country between Mt. Sopris and the Roaring Fork Valley is mainly underlain by gray Mancos Shale (19), a 5000-foot-thick deposit of mud washed eastward by streams flowing off the Western Cordilleran Range, which rose in the Great Basin region between 150 and 100 million years ago. From about 105 million to 70 million years ago, a broad, shallow seaway extended from the Arctic Ocean, through Aspen, to the Gulf of Mexico, and it was in that seaway that the Mancos Shale was deposited. The Cretaceous Seaway had a restricted circulation with little oxygen, and a correspondingly impoverished fauna.

Looking downvalley (west-northwest), you are actually looking across the Elk Mountain gravity glide sheet, in which another synclinal trough, much broader and larger than the one on Ajax, has been formed (Plate 12A). The axis of this trough lies along the Roaring Fork Valley, and the trough itself was formed by uplifts on either side of the valley. To the southwest, uplift was caused by the intrusion of White Rock Granodiorite (22) into the Elk Range 34 million years ago, while to the northeast, uplift occurred along the Castle Creek fault zone, a major break in the Earth's crust which borders the Sawatch Range along Castle Creek south of Aspen, but then veers westward down the Roaring Fork Valley. Mancos Shale has been preserved from erosion in the center of the trough.

Beyond the Mancos hills, a broad, high plateau rises to the skyline (Plate 12A). This is the White River uplift, part of a long, gentle upwarp that extends from the Uinta Mountains in northeast Utah to the Elk Range. It was formed between about 50 and 45 million years ago. Its surface is blanketed with up to 900 feet of basaltic lava flows erupted between 23 and 8 million years ago.

Basalt Mountain, the massive, rounded peak to the right of the plateau, is a basaltic shield volcano. It erupted about 9 million years ago, spilling its fluid basalt lava out on the old Rocky Mountain erosion surface, an extensive plain that once stretched unbroken from the Colorado Plateau eastward across the Continental Divide to blend with the Great Plains. The level of the Rocky Mountain erosion surface is still preserved on the summits of Red and Smuggler mountains north and east of Aspen (Plates 1B and 6A).

Just northwest of Basalt Mountain, another basalt flow, dated at about 8 million years old, lies on a broad valley surface cut by the Roaring Fork up to 2000 feet below the Rocky Mountain erosion surface. This old valley floor is rather poorly preserved on the west slope of Red Mountain below the summit surface and above the glacial outwash terraces at the base. The presence of the 8-million-year-old lava flow on this valley surface shows that the valley must have been cut before the eruption. Because the valley cuts below the 9-million-year-old flow, it must therefore have been formed in the interval between 8 and 9 million years ago. Near

Glenwood Springs, river gravels on top of a 10- to 11-million-year-old basalt flow high on a mesa top give the first evidence of the existence of the Colorado River drainage system. Before then, the climate was too dry to support a major throughgoing river, draining to the sea. Since its inception, this drainage has progressively incised itself deeper below the old Rocky Mountain erosion surface. The modern gorge of the Roaring Fork, cut 1000 to 2000 feet below the broad valley surface, was formed within the past 1.5 million years. A basalt flow of that age on the broad valley surface near Woody Creek has been cut through by the gorge.

Just beyond the north end of the west ridge of Ajax Mountain is a low, sagebrush-covered ridge rising from the flat ground of the valley floor (Plates 7A and 12A). This is a recessional moraine (30) deposited when the retreat of the Second Valley glacier was temporarily halted just southeast of the airport. Both the Oldest and the Second Valley glaciations were more extensive than were the Third and Youngest Valley glaciations. This recessional moraine ridge is therefore farther downvalley than is the terminal moraine of the Third Valley glacier just east of Aspen.

Second Valley lateral moraine, deposited at the side of the glacier, is visible in the prominent terrace at the foot of Red Mountain across the valley (Plate 12A). The hummocky, aspen-covered terrain in Aspen east of the bend of the Roaring Fork is the terminal moraine of the Third Valley glacier (Plate 12B). Outwash gravel and sand, washed downvalley by streams from the melting Third Valley glacier, form the broad plain that stretches from Aspen toward the northwest (Plate 12A). The Second Valley recessional moraine was partially buried by, and rises above, this outwash plain.

The Roaring Fork River and its tributaries have cut narrow gorges in the outwash plain (Plate 12A). These increase in depth downvalley. The course of Maroon Creek shows up as a band of darker vegetation this side of the recessional moraine. A similar, but wider band at the west edge of town marks the course of Castle Creek. The deepening gorge of the Roaring Fork extends northwestward toward Basalt Mountain.

The sharp, steep ridge in the valley floor just west of Aspen is Red Butte (Plate 12A). Before the Second Valley glaciation, Red Butte was a more rounded hill, projecting from the southwest side of Red Mountain. Then the hill was buried in Second Valley glacial moraine. When the Roaring Fork River cut down through the moraine after the glacier melted, a bend of the river happened to be located above the north side of the buried hill. The river was therefore obliged to cut its channel down through both the soft moraine and the more resistant bedrock, thereby isolating the hill from Red Mountain, and eroding away most of its northeast slope.

The rocks of Red Butte (13 through 19) were deposited between about 243 million and 75 million years ago. Their origins and history are covered in detail in the log of the Rio Grande Trail. Beginning about 72 million years ago, when the uplift of the Sawatch Range began, the Earth's crust fractured along what is known as the Castle Creek fault zone. The country east of Aspen has been uplifted as much as 26,000 feet since then, while the rocks in the fault zone have been broken and turned steeply upwards. At Red Butte, they were actually overturned through an angle of 140 degrees, so they are now upside down. The fault zone runs approximately north-south here, and measures from half a mile to a mile across.

Red Mountain dominates the view to the north of Aspen (Plate 1B). Actually, this is a mountain only in a negative sense, in view of the previously mentioned fact that its broad, flat summit once formed part of the Rocky Mountain erosion surface. Remnants of this old land surface can be seen stretching from the top of Smuggler Mountain, northeast of Aspen (Plate 6A), westward toward Basalt Mountain, which rises above it (Plate 12A). On this lookout, you are standing about 500 feet below the old surface, which is poorly preserved on Ajax Mountain.

A remarkable bit of evidence for this old "mountain-top valley bottom" is present on the summits of both Red and Smuggler mountains in the form of Ice Cap glacial moraine (27). This is the oldest moraine in the district, probably about 3 million years old, and it could only have been deposited on mountaintops if the mountains weren't there at the time of its deposition. That is to say, the moraine was laid down on a flat or gently rolling plain by a broad ice sheet flowing westward from the Continental Divide. The ice sheet didn't extend much farther west than Aspen, as is evident from the presence of Ice Cap outwash gravel (28) on ridgetops and terrace remnants between Aspen and Basalt.

Some of these ridgetops and terrace remnants are part of the 8- to 9-million-year-old broad valley surface mentioned above, so this glaciation must have occurred since the broad valley was cut, but its deposits are not present in the deep gorge. This and other evidence pertaining to the 1.5-million-year-old basalt eruption near Woody Creek show that the Ice Cap deposits must be older than that eruption. A remnant of the broad valley surface is present on the west flank of Red Mountain, as mentioned above.

Since the Ice Cap glaciation, then, up to 2000 feet of valley deepening below the broad valley surface has taken place. Both the glaciation and the valley deepening are responses to a broad, regional uplift of the western United States within the last 10 million years. Arizona's Grand Canyon is another. The uplift raised the Rockies high into the colder regions of the atmosphere. This favored the accumulation of snow to form glacial ice, and initiated the Colorado River drainage system, as mentioned previously. Since then, the formerly rather unimpressive topography of this region has been extensively altered by stream and glacial erosion, producing the spectacular modern scenery of the Rockies.

Following the Ice Cap glaciation, subsequent glaciers were confined to the valleys in their downstream portions. Outwash gravel of the first of these, the Oldest Valley, is visible as a broad terrace on the west end of Red Mountain (Plate 12A). The linear, horizontal scars of two irrigation ditches bracket the terrace and extend eastward into Oldest Valley glacial moraine (30). A lower terrace, just visible over the summit of Red Butte (not Red Mountain) is outwash gravel of Second Valley age, while Third Valley outwash forms the extensive valley flats on which the town of Aspen and the airport are located. Youngest Valley outwash is restricted to the modern gorge of the Roaring Fork, cut below the Third Valley outwash surface. This sequence clearly illustrates the fact that valley deepening has continued through time, since each younger outwash deposit lies at a lower level than the next older one.

The red rock of Red Mountain (Plate 1B) is the Maroon Formation (12), deposited between about 293 and 270 million years ago. At that time, flash floods poured mud, silt and gravel into the Central Colorado Trough, from the high Ancestral Front Range to the east and the Ancestral Uncompahgre Range to the southwest. Aspen lay just south of the equator then, and the climate was arid, but subject to occasional violent hurricanes, which produced the flash flooding. The Maroon sediments accumulated to a total thickness of over three miles.

Hunter Creek separates Red Mountain from Smuggler Mountain on the east (Plate 6A). Smuggler is composed of 1.47-billion-year-old quartz monzonite, the same rock that makes up the bulk of Ajax Mountain. The Hunter Creek Valley, then, separates very old rocks on the east from much younger rocks on the west. In fact, there is a very sharp flexure in the Earth's crust at this point, along which the Sawatch Range was uplifted. Largely hidden under Second Valley moraine on the west face of Smuggler Mountain are the steeply upturned layers of eight sedimentary formations (4 through 11) deposited after the intrusion of the quartz monzonite but before the deposition of the Maroon Formation.

Some of the highest grade silver, lead, and zinc ores found in the Aspen district were taken from these formations in the Smuggler and Molly Gibson mines on Smuggler Mountain, including a nugget of pure native silver that weighed over a ton. Mine roads and dumps from these old workings are still evident on this slope, one of the few places remaining where the effects of mining have not been erased by new growth of vegetation. Old photographs of Aspen show an alarming degree of environmental destruction related to these intensive mining operations. The area was virtually devegetated, and it is certainly remarkable and comforting to see that in about 50 years the environment has recovered so completely.

Beyond the Smuggler mines, the valley of Hunter Creek is noteworthy in that it drops rather suddenly in a steep cascade to the Roaring Fork. This situation is a result of more intensive and rapid deepening of the Roaring Fork Valley by glaciation than occurred in the valley of Hunter Creek, in which smaller, tributary glaciers flowed. Hanging glacial valleys of this sort are fairly common in the Sawatch and Elk mountains east and southwest of Aspen.

Notice the course of the Roaring Fork River through the Third Valley terminal moraine east of town (Plate 12B). Where the river cuts across the moraine, its bed is steep and bouldery, but in the alluvial floodplain behind the moraine (and in a small alluvial pocket within the moraine itself), the channel is gently graded, meandering, and filled with sand, silt, and mud (Plate 13A). In general, the accumulation of fine-grained sediment in a segment of river channel indicates that the river is no longer downcutting in that segment. The large boulders in the remaining segments here were derived from the surrounding glacial moraine.

In the grassy pasture of the floodplain east of the terminal moraine, several meander scars are evident, some with ponds in them. These mark former positions of the channel of the Roaring Fork.

On the valley wall above the floodplain, you can see a hanging glacial valley, and just beyond it two rather prominent, but narrow, horizontal benches (Plate 13A). The lower of these benches is the lateral moraine ridge of the Third Valley glacier, and it shows the height to which the glacier filled the Roaring Fork Valley. The upper bench is the lip of the bedrock valley cut by the Second Valley glacier. This lip is about 2000 feet above the present valley floor. Stream and glacial erosion have deepened the Roaring Fork Valley by this amount within the past 1.5 million years, following a general uplift of the land that many years ago.

Rio Grande Trail

½ day, 1½ miles; elevation loss 140 feet from Cemetery Lane Bridge at 7720 feet to end of log at 7580 feet.

USGS Topographic Quadrangle Map: Aspen
USGS Geologic Quadrangle Map: Aspen GQ-933.

Access: Drive west out of Aspen on Colorado State Highway 82. Cross the Castle Creek Bridge and turn right at the traffic light onto Cemetery Lane. Follow this for 1.2 miles down to the Roaring Fork River just east of Red Butte; cross the bridge and park in the lot on the left. The trail begins here and follows the north bank of the Roaring Fork River westward along the old Denver and Rio Grande Western Railroad bed.

Stop 1: *Trailhead*

The small patch of flattish ground to the north of the river where the trail begins is underlain by recent deposits of the Roaring Fork. The pond, of course, is man-made.

Across the river, the steep northeast slope of Red Butte is composed mainly of reddish shale and sandstone of the State Bridge Formation (13). This rock unit was deposited here about 243 to 215 million years ago as sand, mud, and minor gravel from various sources, both local and distant. Rockfall debris from the steep slope has accumulated at the base of Red Butte.

To the north, in the middle distance, is a slope formed on glacial moraine (30) of the Second Valley glaciation (Plate 15B). Note the huge, rounded boulders, and the flattish top of this deposit. This moraine is a heterogeneous assemblage of such boulders together with gravel, sand, silt, and clay derived from a variety of rock types eroded from higher parts of the Roaring Fork watershed by the Second Valley glacier. There is evidence for one earlier and two later valley glaciations in the Roaring Fork, but the Second Valley appears to have been the most extensive.

The slope in the close foreground to the northwest is in the Gothic Formation (10), a mixture of sandstone, shale, and limestone representing material eroded from the Ancestral Uncompahgre uplift as it rose southwest of Aspen about 300 million years ago. A major fault passes between this slope and Red Butte, running north-

northwesterly through the spot where you are standing. The country east of the fault has been raised as much as 26,000 feet since about 72 million years ago, thereby forming the high Sawatch Range, which includes Colorado's highest mountain peaks. West of the fault, younger rocks are exposed at the surface. Here, at Red Butte, these rocks have actually been turned upside down by rotation of a large block between this fault and another, parallel fault about half a mile to the west. These two faults define the boundaries of the Castle Creek fault zone.

Stop 2: *Beyond green metal gate*

The flat, silty ground of the river floodplain has given way here to a steep, hummocky terrain in compact earth material that ranges in size from clay to rounded boulders of a variety of rock types. The flat railroad grade has been cut through this material, which is glacial moraine (30) of the Second Valley glaciation. Notice the large boulders in the river bed (Plate 14A). These have been washed out of the moraine and they are too large to be moved downriver by major floods.

Stop 3: *Mouth of Slaughterhouse Creek*

The railroad cut has created a waterfall on the steep channel of Slaughterhouse Creek here. The creek is responding to this disturbance by building a small alluvial fan across the cut. Rock particles that are small enough to be moved by the current of a flood on the creek will be transported across the fan into the Roaring Fork River. Particles that are too big to be moved by a flood will remain on the fan, thus building it higher and steeper. But the steeper it gets, the more gravity assists the flow of water in moving the larger particles, so eventually a stable slope must be established on the fan.

The cutbank here is an excellent place to observe the characteristics of typical glacial moraine: heterogeneous rock types and sizes, and glacially smoothed and rounded boulders.

Along the trail beyond the Slaughterhouse Creek crossing are several large, mostly angular boulders of diverse rock types. Such rocks, whose place of origin is unknown, and probably unknowable, are referred to by geologists as "float." In this case, since no known geologic process seems adequate to explain the distribution of the float, it may be assumed that human activity was responsible. Some of these large boulders are granodiorite (2), with dark amphibole and biotite, light, chalky feldspar and gray, glassy quartz. Some are of sandstone, probably derived from the Entrada Sandstone (15), which you will encounter a little farther on. On a few of these boulders are joints, or fracture surfaces, coated with veins of pyrite, an iron sulfide. Chemical weathering of the pyrite has formed yellowish to reddish stains of limonite, a hydrous iron oxide.

A little farther along the left side of the trail are several brown mudstone boulders, probably from the State Bridge Formation (13), one of which exposes a bedding plane with well-developed, symmetrical ripple marks (Plate 14B). These indicate that the muddy sediment in which they were formed was deposited in shallow water that was subjected to gentle agitation by wind.

Also on the left is a large, rounded boulder of contorted biotite gneiss (1) of a type known as *migmatite,* in which igneous magma has been injected between the foliation planes of the gneiss under high pressure (Plate 8A). Minerals present in this rock include pinkish feldspar, clear, flaky muscovite mica, dark, flaky biotite mica, reddish garnet, and gray, vitreous quartz.

Stop 4: *Just beyond second small stream crossing*

Across the Roaring Fork River is a steep bank of red shale and greenish-white, sandy limestone in layers which stand out from the shale due to their greater resistance to erosion. This is the Chinle Formation (14), which was originally laid down about 200 million years ago as mud and volcanic ash derived from mountain uplifts mainly to the southwest. The railroad cutbank ahead on the right is also in Chinle Formation. As with the underlying State Bridge (13) and the overlying Entrada, Morrison, Burro Canyon, Dakota and Mancos formations (15 through 19), the Chinle is overturned here, in the Castle Creek fault zone, 140 degrees away from its originally horizontal position.

Stop 5: *Opposite the middle of the same cutbank*

Across the river, the contact between the Chinle Formation and the Entrada Sandstone (15) may be seen. The Entrada, being younger than the Chinle, was of course deposited on top of the Chinle, but here the Entrada lies below the Chinle because of the overturning of the stratigraphy in the Castle Creek fault zone. The Entrada Sandstone was originally laid down as a deposit of beach sand at the edge of the Sundance Sea, which advanced southward over Aspen from Canada about 160 million years ago. The contact between these two formations can also be seen in the railroad cutbank where the soil color changes from red to buff. High upon the slope to the right (north) a prominent pinnacle of Entrada Sandstone rises above the surrounding country (Plates 14A and 15B).

Stop 6: *Opposite Entrada Sandstone pinnacle on right*

Across the river is another geologic contact, here between the Entrada Sandstone and the Morrison Formation (16) (Plate 15A). This contact is gradational and indefinite, but it represents a rather radical change in the geologic environment of the western United States. In response to the newly initiated westward drift of North America over the Pacific Ocean floor, the Western Cordilleran mountain range was uplifted from Alaska through Mexico about 150 million years ago. Mud, sand, and volcanic ash were washed and blown eastward from this high range to accumulate, in the low-lying Rocky Mountain region, as the varicolored shales, limestones, and sandstones of the Morrison Formation. Greenish to purplish colors in the sediment suggest that the Morrison muds may have been laid down in a lagoonal environment that was alternately flooded by the sea and exposed to the air.

Stop 7: *Sandstone rockfall in the railroad bed*

Obviously, this large rockfall happened in recent years since the railroad bed was abandoned (Plate 15B). Look up the slope to see the landslide path and a fresh-looking scar in the sandstone crag from which the material of the rockfall broke loose. Several of the fallen boulders in the trail have smoothly polished, grooved surfaces on them in various places. These are called *slickensides*, and they are evidence of faulting in the rocks. The grooves indicate the direction of relative movement along the fault. It's usually possible to tell whether the fault went "up" or "down" the grooves by feeling the surface for very slight differences in roughness going one way and then the other. These minor faults are related to the largescale Castle Creek fault zone mentioned before.

Ripplemarks are also present in some of these rocks, suggesting that the Entrada Sandstone was at least in part waterlaid, although ripplemarks can also be formed by wind.

On a few of the boulders, bluish copper stain (probably chrysocolla, a copper silicate) is present along with mosslike stains of manganese dioxide (pyrolusite) and yellowish to reddish iron oxide (limonite). These mineral deposits are all indicative of iron, manganese, and copper bearing solutions that invaded the rocks of the Aspen area during the Earth movements that produced the faulting on this western border of the Sawatch Range.

Stop 8: *Prominent sandstone crag cut by railroad passageway*

Looking back toward the rockfall, you will notice a shallow valley between the Entrada crag and the crag above you (Plate 15B). This valley was eroded in the weaker Morrison Formation between the more resistant sandstone formations to the east and west of it.

A large boulder is perched on the Entrada crag above the rockfall scar. This is a *glacial erratic* that was deposited there by the Second Valley glacier in the Roaring Fork. It shows that at the time of that glaciation, Red Butte was practically or completely buried by glacial moraine. Prior to that glaciation, the Roaring Fork must have flowed to the south of Red Butte, at a higher level than that of its present bed. At that time, Red Butte was a low, rounded hill projecting from the southwest flank of Red Mountain. After the butte was buried in Second Valley glacial moraine, the Roaring Fork River happened to reestablish itself north of its former position, and as it cut down through the moraine to, and below, its former level, it also cut down through the rocks of the north side of Red Butte, thereby isolating it from Red Mountain.

The crag above you is in the Dakota Sandstone (18). Between the Dakota and the Morrison is another, poorly exposed formation, the Burro Canyon (17), a mixture of conglomerate, sandstone, and shale washed eastward by streams flowing off mountain uplifts in Utah about 108 million years ago. These uplifts were a continuation, farther east, of earlier uplifts in the Western Cordillera. In general, the history of this great mountain chain involved a progressive eastward development of mountain building activity. The fact that the sedimentary particles of the Burro Canyon are generally coarser than those of the Morrison reflects the greater proximity of this new mountain uplift to Aspen than the uplift which produced the Morrison Formation. Local uplifts in central Colorado also contributed to the Burro Canyon.

The Dakota, like the Entrada, was originally a beach sand. About 103 million years ago, the Rocky Mountain region began to sink as the country to the west continued to rise, and a vast seaway developed, splitting the continent from the Gulf of Mexico to the Arctic Ocean. The Dakota Sandstone was deposited as beach dune sand as this Western Interior Seaway advanced on the Rocky Mountain region from both north and south.

In the cut and blasted portion of the outcrop, notice the abundance of small intersecting faults, which offset thin layers of dark, carbonaceous shale within the sandstone. Smoke from steam locomotives blackens the outcrop.

Stop 9: *Cutbank in dark gray shale on right, about 100 feet west of Dakota Sandstone crag*

As the Western Interior Seaway deepened, mud accumulated on its floor above the Dakota Sandstone. The sources of this mud were the streams that flowed eastward off the Western Cordillera. In time, the mud became compacted and indurated into the mile-thick Mancos Shale exposed here, which dominates much of the landscape to the northwest of Aspen, especially in the Snowmass Creek area.

Stop 10: *Beaver pond*

This is an active beaver pond which differs from most beaver ponds in that it wasn't created by beavers. A bend of the Roaring Fork River made the cut in which the pond sits, and the railroad embankment now isolates it from the river. A beaver lodge, constructed of cottonwood sticks, is situated at the west end of the pond. Voles—small, mouselike rodents—are quite abundant here.

The steep slope above and to the west of the pond is part of the *recessional moraine* of the Second Valley glacier. As the glacier was receding—melting faster at its terminus than it was growing downvalley—the terminus "stood still" here during a cold spell of several years' duration, while the glacier gradually built a large ridge of moraine across the Roaring Fork Valley.

Across the river from the beaver pond is a bank of Mancos Shale with several interlayered beds of limestone, one of which causes a small waterfall (Plate 16A). The eddying current of the river at this point has carved several small caves from the soft shale. This particular bed has a drag fold, or wrinkle, in it, which indicates, by its shape, that the rocks to the west moved upward relative to those on the east. If you own a copy of John Denver's *Rocky Mountain High* record album, you may recognize this spot as the setting for the cover picture.

A fantastically contorted blue spruce hangs onto a precarious perch to the left of the folded limestone bed.

Stop 11: *Confluence of Roaring Fork River and Maroon Creek*

Maroon Creek drains the high Elk Range to the southwest of Aspen. The cobbles in the alluvial gravel at this stream junction are the largest rocks that major floods on the Roaring Fork or Maroon Creek are capable of moving.

The flat-topped bluff above and downstream of the

confluence is composed of glacial outwash gravel deposited during the melting of the Third Valley glacier.

Stop 12: *Huge boulders in glacial moraine on right*

This is the heart of the Second Valley recessional moraine, the southern part of which is visible across the river, rising above the Third Valley glacial outwash in which it lies partially buried. These large boulders in the moraine have been smoothed and rounded by transportation downvalley within and beneath the glacier (Plate 16B). One boulder of light quartz monzonite (3) contains several inclusions of darker rock which may be fragments of the old biotite gneiss (1) country rock into which the quartz monzonite was intruded. The huge boulders in the riverbed below you rolled into their present positions from the moraine above the river. They are much too large to be moved by river floods. Smaller boulders that *are* capable of being moved by floodwaters are present among the larger ones in the river channel.

Just beyond the large boulders in the railroad cut is an outcrop of Mancos Shale in which the bedding planes lie horizontally except on the eastern end of the outcrop, where they are tilted upward sharply toward the vertical. This outcrop presents somewhat of a geological enigma. One possible interpretation is that it is an enormous, loose block of Mancos surrounded by moraine, and that the pressure of ice-thrusting on its eastern end caused the warping of the bedding planes, but the location of the outcrop on the trace of the western branch of the Castle Creek fault zone makes it more likely that the block only appears to be surrounded by moraine, but is actually in place, and that the bedding planes have been upturned by movement on the fault. We prefer the latter interpretation.

Stop 13: *Next cutbank on right*

Notice the difference between this slope material and that which formed the last cutbank. The range of rock particle sizes has been greatly reduced. While morainal material ranges from clay to boulders, this deposit has a narrower size range: silt to cobbles, with a *mode*, or characteristic diameter, of about 6 inches. This is glacial outwash gravel of the Third Valley glaciation (31). The town of Aspen and the airport are located on the flat upper surface of this extensive deposit.

Stop 14: *Waterfall over a cliff in Mancos Shale*

This rather slimy-looking deposit is a mixture of algae

and travertine (calcium carbonate precipitated from the streamwater). Across the Roaring Fork River, the Third Valley outwash gravel surface is well displayed, as is the Second Valley recessional moraine rising above it (Plate 7A). The gorge cut within the outwash gravel by the Roaring Fork River deepens downvalley and then gradually becomes shallower again, indicating that the present gradient along the river is more concave upward than is the gradient on the outwash where the river flowed before cutting its present gorge. Variations in the shape of stream profiles are determined by the requirements of moving water and weathered rock debris off the land so that they don't accumulate. Gravity assists in this process. Where streamflow is low, channel profiles are steep to take advantage of this gravity-assist. This is why stream gradients tend to be steep in desert regions and gentle in humid areas where streamflow is much greater. Naturally, if streamflow increases downvalley, gradients will flatten in proportion to produce an overall concave channel profile. This is characteristic of humid areas, in which water tables are high enough to feed the streams. Under these conditions, little water is lost from the streams as they flow toward the ocean, and the flow increases with the addition of each tributary downstream. In arid regions, water tables are rarely high or persistent enough to feed the streams, and water loss downstream by percolation is usually enough to offset additions by tributaries. As a result, channel profiles are much less concave, since flow doesn't increase much downstream.

Obviously, flow was much higher during the glacialoutburst floods that deposited the Third Valley outwash than it is now in the Roaring Fork. Why, then, is the river channel gradient gentler and more concave than the outwash? The answer to this enigma lies in the far greater sediment load that the outburst floods had to transport than what the modern Roaring Fork River carries when it is in flood. The more debris a stream has to carry, the steeper its gradient must be, again because of the need for a gravity-assist in moving the material. (A general equation describing the whole situation, for those who appreciate the succinctness of a mathematical description, is $S = kM_a D_b / Q_c$, where S is stream gradient at a given point, M is the mass and D the average diameter of transported sediment, Q is the streamflow rate, and a, b, c and k are empirical constants which vary under different climatic and lithologic environments.)

From here, the trail continues toward Woody Creek, but it has few geologic features not already covered up to this point. One noteworthy item is a U.S. Geological Survey Mesozoic Fossil locality, number D 6029, on the Mancos Shale cliff in the hollow of the next major bend in the trail.

Buckskin Pass Trail

1 day, 3¼ miles; elevation gain 2870 feet from Maroon Lake Campground at 9592 feet to Buckskin Pass at 12,462 feet.

USGS Topographic Quadrangle Map: Maroon Bells
USGS Geologic Quadrangle Map: Maroon Bells GQ-788.

Access: Drive 11.5 miles up Maroon Creek Road from its intersection with Colorado State 82, just west of Aspen, to Maroon Lake Campground. Park in the parking lot overlooking Maroon Lake and the Maroon Bells. The trail starts above the west side of Maroon Lake, and proceeds directly toward the Maroon Bells (Plate 17A).

Stop 1: Trailhead at parking area

Due south, directly across Maroon Lake, is Pyramid Peak, carved by stream and glacial erosion from nearly horizontal beds of the 293- to 270-million-year-old Maroon Formation (12). This rock unit, composed of sandstone, shale, limestone, and conglomerate, was originally laid down by violent floods that flowed into the Central Colorado Trough from ranges of the Ancestral Rocky Mountains to the east and the southwest. More than a three-mile thickness of these sediments accumulated in the Trough, attesting to the rapid erosion of these high ranges under the extremely hot and dry, but hurricane-prone climate of the time. The Maroon Formation is usually dark red in color, as it is in the pinnacles on the skyline ridge to the northwest, but on Pyramid Peak it has been turned into a greenish-gray metamorphic rock called hornfels. This change took place during the intrusion of the White Rock Granodiorite (22), which produced a large, domelike uplift in the Elk Range southwest of Aspen approximately 34 million years ago.

Nearer Aspen, the Maroon Formation strata dip northward at about a 30-degree angle. The fact that they are nearly horizontal here shows that Pyramid Peak and the Maroon Bells are near the crest of the uplift.

The granodiorite intrusion took place along the Elk Range thrust, a nearly horizontal plane surface underlying the Elk Mountains and cropping out on the eastern and western edges of the range. Seventy-two million years ago, when the Sawatch Range was uplifted by vertical forces to the east, a great sheet of sedimentary rocks, some 20 by 50 miles in area and about five miles thick, detached itself from the steep west flank of the Sawatch uplift and slid westward upon the soft, weak shales of the 313- to 300-million-year-old Belden Formation (9). This enormous *gravity glide sheet* now blankets most of the country immediately west of Aspen.

Directly below the highest visible pinnacle on Pyramid Peak (this is not the summit) is a small remnant of lateral glacial moraine (30), which has been falling into the lake, forming a lightly vegetated cone of talus or rockfall debris. Lateral moraine is a deposit of heterogeneous rock types and sizes dragged along by a moving glacier and deposited at its sides.

The lake itself was formed by extensive mudflow and talus deposits (32) that fell from the glacially over-steepened sedimentary rock of the valley walls. The classic U-shape of a glaciated valley is clearly shown by Maroon Creek canyon south of the lake (Plate 17). This shape has been somewhat modified by mudflows, especially to the west. Mudflow deposits cover most of the west wall of the valley, and they underlie the Maroon Lake Campground. Three prominent gullies feed the large debris fan just upvalley from the campground (Plate 17B). Dark lines of vegetation on this steep, grassy slope outline the positions of stream courses. Frequent snow avalanches keep the meadows clear of all but herbaceous vegetation.

Beyond Maroon Lake and in front of the base of the Maroon Bells is a sparsely vegetated, flat-topped deposit of coarse, angular rockfall debris that probably fell from the west face of Pyramid Peak (Plate 12A). This deposit has impounded the drainage of West Maroon Creek, thereby forming the basin of Crater Lake.

Like Pyramid Peak, the Maroon Bells are composed of Maroon Formation, metamorphosed to greenish hornfels near the base where the rock is closer to the underlying igneous intrusives.

A large rock glacier is perched on a broad shelf below the imposing north face of North Maroon Peak. Rock glaciers are rather enigmatic deposits of boulders that have the general form and behavior of glaciers, but are composed of rock rather than ice. The mechanism that causes them to move appears to be the slow flow of interstitial ice that persists among the boulders of the deposit.

Stop 2: *Near edge of clearing in aspens opposite southwest end of Maroon Lake*

The dead aspens on the slope above you were probably

killed by the airblast of a powder snow avalanche, which tore the new buds from the branches. Young sprouts are arising from the network of aspen roots that lies shallowly buried amid the rockfall debris and organic mulch on the forest floor.

Stop 3: *Rocky slope with young aspens leaning downhill*

These aspens have been pushed over by snow avalanches. Across the valley, on the west face of Pyramid Peak, a large cone of rock debris has accumulated at the base of a prominent rockslide chute. The cone is largely vegetated, but an irregular channel runs down its left side, indicating recent slide activity.

Stop 4: *Forest Service signboard on right in aspen forest*

The rocks that make up the landslide deposits on the forest floor here are Maroon Formation (12), slightly metamorphosed from their original bright red siltstones to a gray-green argillite. The slight glitter in the rocks comes from tiny flakes of sericite, a form of muscovite mica derived from the alteration of orthoclase feldspar. A persistent slaty cleavage is present in the argillite. If this were better developed, through stronger metamorphism, the rock would be considered to be a slate.

Stop 5: *Rockslide path on right with large boulders; open rockslide slope just beyond*

The boulders in this slide path are a mixture of Maroon argillite and granodiorite porphyry (22), a light gray-green igneous rock with crystals of pinkish feldspar. Several of the boulders, including the biggest one, are composed of both rock types. Notice, on the largest boulder, how the igneous porphyry has sent offshooots of itself into the surrounding argillite.

This deposit of sliderock, or talus, has been stabilized by a fairly mature growth of aspen. The curving of the tree bases, caused by slow downhill creep of the talus, is called *pistol-butting*.

Stop 6: *Open rockslide slope*

The recency of this rockslide is indicated by three things: several young aspens have had their lower trunks buried by sliderock; there is little vegetation on the lower part of the slope; and the rocks of the slide are not covered with a growth of lichen. The young aspens below the trail were not bent over by rockfall, but by snow avalanche.

Stop 7: *Large clearing with scattered spruce trees; flat-topped bench of loose, jagged rocks ahead*

This is the large rockfall deposit visible above Maroon Lake from the parking lot (Plate 17). The extreme jaggedness of the rocks in this deposit (32) distinguishes it from glacial moraine (30), which it otherwise resembles. Morainal boulders are generally rounded by abrasion in transit within and beneath glaciers. The west face of Pyramid Peak, with its rather rotten-looking rock, is probably the source area for the rockfall, which may have resulted from the collapse of a large pinnacle.

Stop 8: *Trail switchbacks up rockfall*

Charred, fallen trees and sparse lichen cover indicate that a major fire occurred here recently. Fire is a natural part of the environment, usually caused by lightning strikes, but also by the spontaneous combustion of rotting wood and possibly by rockfall. Manmade fires have become proportionately more important in the Rockies since the latter 1800's.

Stop 9: *Fork in trail, sign post*

The rockfall deposit ends here at this trail junction. Before the rockfall occurred, West Maroon Creek flowed down this valley to its confluence with East Maroon Creek about two miles below Maroon Lake. This flow was interrupted by the rockfall, which ponded the drainage upvalley, thereby forming Crater Lake, which is visible to the south of the trail intersection (Plate 18A). Crater Lake has no surface outlet, but a fair amount of water flows under the rockfall debris. If this were not happening, the level of Crater Lake would rise about another 70 feet until it overtopped the rockfall deposit and spilled over into the valley below. This may in fact happen eventually, since the lake is rapidly filling with silt at its upstream end. If this silt proceeds to seal the leaks in the lake bottom, the water level will begin to rise.

This is a good vantage from which to view the large rock glacier, mentioned previously, at the base of the steep north face of North Maroon Peak.

Beyond Crater Lake, extensive cones of rockslide debris cover the lower valley walls below Pyramid Peak and the Maroon Bells (Plate 18A). These deposits are filling in the U-shaped trough left by the Youngest Valley glacier in the easily eroded siltstones and argillites of the Maroon Formation.

Take the right fork; a little farther on, take another right at a sign, on the left, which points to Snowmass Trail. The ascent from here is consistently fairly steep.

Stop 10: *Slope of dead aspen and bent-over spruce and fir*

This is a snow avalanche path. The aspens on the slope to the right were probably killed by airblast from large powder snow avalanches.

Stop 11: *Straight section of trail on a steep, east-facing, forested slope; narrow ridge below and parallel with trail*

The ridge below the trail is a lateral moraine deposited at the west edge of a glacier that flowed down the West Maroon Creek valley. Notice the rounded rock fragments on this ridge and compare these with the angular fragments of the landslide material on the steep slope above you. Rounded cobbles and boulders are characteristic of glacial moraine.

Stop 12: *First half-mile sign*

Here, the trail turns right, up the glaciated valley of Minnehaha Creek. On the right hand hillslope, the rockfall deposits have given way to glacial moraine deposited by the Youngest Valley glacier that flowed down Minnehaha Gulch from Buckskin and Willow passes. Notice the hummocky terrain (Plate 18B).

A good view may be had from here of the silt deposits that are gradually filling up Crater Lake on its southwest end.

Stop 13: *Junction with a small side trail to left in a meadow*

The large boulders at the junction are quartz pebble conglomerate, probably derived from the upper part of the Maroon Formation. Such conglomerates indicate one or more of three things: either the source area from which they were eroded was very close by, or the flood that deposited them, as gravels, was especially violent and far-reaching, or there was a sudden, strong mountain uplift somewhere in the region. The last of these, or a combination of the last two, is most likely, since the nearest known source areas were the Ancestral Front Range to the east and the Ancestral Uncompahgre Range to the southwest.

Stop 14: *Sharp right bend in trail; deep, rocky gorge to left*

Minnehaha Creek used to flow in a channel several hundred feet to the left of where it is now in this deep gorge. A rockfall upvalley diverted the creek toward the east side of the valley, where it cut this narrow gorge through glacial moraine and bedrock. A tributary stream enters from the left, and this has also formed a gorge according to the principle that two intersecting streams should have their mouths at the same elevation.

Stop 15: *Trail crosses Minnehaha Creek*

To the right, above the trail, is a thick deposit of rock debris which formed a dam, mentioned previously, across Minnehaha Gulch. This is the upper part of the deep, narrow gorge you saw below. Above the trail, it has cut down through the dam, and the gorge continues in bedrock below the trail. The bedrock here is Maroon Formation, metamorphosed to quartzitic hornfels by an intrusive body of 34-million-year-old granodiorite (22) which forms the core of the hill you have been climbing. The rusty color of the rock comes from the decomposition of pyrite, an iron disulfide disseminated through it. The main uplift of the Elk Range occurred at the same time as the granodiorite intrusion.

Stop 16: *Trail enters a V-notch with a small stream in it*

This is a small tributary of Minnehaha Creek. Both this and the main creek have cut channels through a landslide deposit here.

Stop 17: *Top of notch*

The large topographic bowl above you has been carved out of the Maroon Formation by the action of valley glaciers and permanent snowfields. The valley on the right passes northward into the glacial bowl, or *cirque*, that lies to the southeast of Willow Pass. The glaciers that formed in the Willow Pass and Buckskin Pass cirques coalesced at this point to flow as one stream of ice down Minnehaha Gulch.

On the skyline of the cirque above you is Buckskin Pass. You may see a snow cornice still persisting at the pass where winter winds have deposited a thick rim of snow on the leeward side of the pass.

Stop 18: *Fork in trail; stay left*

On the slope to the north, the willows appear to be growing in irregular, horizontal stripes. This is a result of the phenomenon of soil creep, which tends to produce an effect, on steep, unstable slopes, similar to washboards on a gravel road. The willows tend to stabilize these soil ripples.

Stop 19: *Broad, flattish surface below Maroon Bells, in foreground*

This surface is an *alp* (Plate 19A). Like those in

Switzerland, this alp was formed by a glacier grinding a new valley below an older, broader valley bottom. The alp is also visible across the valley to the northeast, where its form is influenced by the attitude of the bedding planes in the Maroon Formation, which are dipping at about 15 degrees to the north.

Large, sparsely vegetated cones of talus flank the ridge to the west.

Stop 20: *Prominent band of light green rock in red Maroon Formation outcrop at trail bend*

This is a *sill* of porphyritic granodiorite (22) that was injected along a bedding plane in the Maroon Formation during the uplift of the Elk Range about 34 million years ago (Plate 19B).

Stop 21: *Below cornice*

The bedrock here is porphyritic granodiorite (Plates 20A and 20B). Notice the large rectangular crystals of pinkish feldspar scattered throughout the otherwise fine-grained rock. Crystals of this type are called *phenocrysts* ("visible crystals"). They are thought to have formed while the magma was cooling very slowly at great depth. Later, when the magma was injected into higher levels of the Earth's crust, the remaining minerals crystallized rather quickly, chilled by the surrounding rock. Since rapid chilling causes many crystallization centers to form where few would form under slow cooling, the resulting crystals are very fine grained.

Stop 22: *Buckskin Pass*

Passes are the meeting places of the headwaters of drainage systems. To the southeast, rainwater and snowmelt run down Minnehaha Gulch and Maroon Creek to the Roaring Fork. To the northwest, they flow down Snowmass Creek, joining the Roaring Fork several miles farther downstream. Erosion may be more active on one side of a pass than on the other, in which case the pass will migrate away from the more intensively eroding side. Here, the deep cirques on the southeast side suggest that Buckskin Pass may have shifted northwestward due to more active glacial erosion in the cirques.

The deposit of jagged, frost-shattered rock on the pass is called *Felsenmeer*, a German term meaning "sea of rocks" (Plate 20B). High mountain regions subject to a vigorous frost climate usually have Felsenmeer well developed on summits and ridgetops.

Just below the pass to the west, a spectacular rock glacier sits in a northwest-facing glacial cirque (Plate 21A). Slow flow of interstitial ice within this great rock pile produces a slow, but inexorable downslope movement within the rock glacier.

The two large peaks to the west are Snowmass Mountain, on the right, and the twin summits of Snowmass and Hagerman peaks on the left. These peaks are made of the same 34-million-year old granodiorite you encountered previously, but here it is exposed at the surface as a large, roughly equidimensional intrusive igneous body known as a *stock*. The Snowmass stock is about nine miles across.

North of the pass is Buckskin Peak with its gentle west face and steep east wall. This steep face was carved on the mountain by a glacier that flowed eastward down the valley of Willow Creek into Minnehaha Gulch.

At Buckskin Pass, you are near the western edge of the Elk Mountain gravity glide sheet. This was, of course, the leading edge of the slide, which threw the strata ahead of it into an enormous fold that ultimately ruptured along its crest, allowing the glide sheet to ride westward as a detached unit. Hidden from view here by a high ridge, of which Snowmass Mountain forms the northwestern end, is the Schofield syncline, part of the overridden, marginal fold which has been exposed by erosion on the western edge of the glide sheet.

Independence Lake Trail

½ day, 5 miles; elevation gain 1300 feet from trailhead at 11,506 feet to Geissler Pass at 12,806 feet.

USGS Topographic Quadrangle Map: Mount Champion

Access: Drive east on Colorado State Highway 82 18.65 miles to a hairpin turn at timberline. Here, a sign on the right marks the place where the road crosses the Roaring Fork River. Park on either side of the road. Take the Lost Man Lake Trail and follow the east bank of the Roaring Fork.

Stop 1: *Trailhead*

A bench, extensively developed here at about 12,500 feet, is clearly visible in the mountainous country to the southeast. The sharp, toothlike summit of Grizzly Peak on the right and the more massive, rounded summit of Blue Mountain on the left, both rise above this bench level on the Continental Divide.

These benches once formed a continuous land surface that stretched both westward and eastward where it merged with the

Great Plains. At that time, the relief of the Rocky Mountains was much more subdued than it is now, with the highest summits rising only 1000 or 2000 feet above this old plain, which has been called the Rocky Mountain erosion surface. The plain was formed during a geologically stable interval after the intensive mountain-building activity of the Laramide orogeny between 72 and 53 million years ago. Since its formation, several broad uplifts of the western United States have occurred, and the rivers of the region have responded to this change by cutting downward, forming deep canyons that account for most of the present topographic relief of the Rocky Mountain region. Only a few remnants of the old land surface remain as these high benches. In Aspen, the flat summits of Red and Smuggler mountains are parts of the Rocky Mountain erosion surface (Plate 6A).

Looking down the Roaring Fork, you can see the typical U-shape of a glaciated valley. On the left, the valley wall has been especially oversteepened due to a bend in the course of the valley. Rockslide cones have begun the slow process of restoring the former gentler slope of the valley wall.

Above you on the west skyline is a sharp V-notch. This is the outlet for Linkins Lake, which sits in a small tributary glacial valley. The trail passes by this lake on its return to the trailhead.

Stop 2: *About 300 yards up the trail; first good view upvalley*

The typical U-shaped cross-profile of a glaciated valley is quite evident here.

Stop 3: *Stream crossing*

The earth material in the valley bottom is glacial ground moraine (30), a mixture of rounded boulders and cobbles, gravel, sand, silt, and clay brought down the valley by glaciers. The stream bed is filled with glacially smoothed and rounded boulders, cobbles, and gravel from which the finer sand, silt, and clay have been washed away by the stream. Some of these larger rocks have also accumulated in the stream channel after creeping slowly down the gentle sideslopes of the shallow swale in which the stream flows. This slow creep results from the action of gravity aided by seasonal freezing and thawing of the ground. It affects the fine-grained material as well as the coarse, but the fines are flushed away by the flowing stream. In time, this process produces a bowl-shaped drainage basin centered on the stream channel.

On the valley wall to your left (west) the process of soil creep is evident in the horizontal stripes of willow growth on the steep slope. These stripes are called soil ripples, and they form under the combined influences of gravity and freeze-thaw cycles.

Stop 4: *Top of the first rise by a rock buttress on the right*

When a glacier flows down through a stream valley, it not only alters the cross-profile of the valley to a U-shape, but it also modifies the long profile. Resistant bedrock tends to remain as high spots, while weaker rock is scoured out to form depressions in the valley floor. Here, where the bedrock is all 1.7-billion-year-old biotite gneiss (1) of fairly consistent resistance to erosion, the difference between weaker and more resistant rock is more likely to be due to the extent to which the rock has been fractured in various places than to differences in rock type. Highly jointed or fractured rock is more amenable to glacial erosion than is massive, unfractured rock.

Here, an outcrop of gneiss on the valley floor illustrates this phenomenon of long profile irregularity. Since the last glacier melted, a few thousand years ago, and the Roaring Fork River began to flow again, the channel has been cut down through this bedrock hump and through the ground moraine that had been deposited on its downstream side by the glacier. Unlike glaciers, streams tend to maintain long profiles that approach mathematically perfect curves. This topic is covered in more detail in the Rio Grande Trail Log.

The hump in the valley floor is properly known as a *riegel*. Its upper surface has been smoothed and polished by the passage of glacial ice. The downstream ends of bedrock outcrops tend to be rather jagged in comparison with their upstream ends because of the plucking action of the glacier as it passed over them.

Stop 5: *Top of second rise*

This is another riegel, also incised by the Roaring Fork River.

Stop 6: *Large swampy bowl in the valley floor*

This is a *springbowl*, in which downslope creep of the water-saturated soil and ground moraine has greatly enlarged a depression below a third riegel in the valley floor (Plate 21B). The abundant moisture for this process is supplied by several springs that emerge at this point in the valley.

Don't follow the trail into the swampy bottom of the springbowl, but begin climbing up the right hand slope toward Blue Mountain (Plate 22B) and follow the rim of the bowl northward to rejoin the trail above. Watch for small springbowls and pocket gopher tunnels on the slope of the main bowl as you go up.

Stop 7: *Rim of spring bowl*

You are on an *alp*. The term often calls to mind a range of rugged, snowy peaks, but actually, alps are gently sloping meadows high above valley bottoms on the shoulders of the peaks. They are remnants of preexisting, high, open valley floors below which glaciers have carved out deeper and narrower valleys. Across the Roaring Fork Valley to the west is an even more striking alp representing the opposite slope of this old, high, open valley (Plate 21B). Above it is a remnant of the Rocky Mountain erosion surface.

Glacial deposits farther downvalley show that there have been at least four episodes of valley glaciation, and at least one ice sheet glacier that covered the Rocky Mountain and broad valley surfaces before the cutting of the deeper valleys.

At the west base of Blue Mountain is a symmetrical cone of talus, or rockslide debris, derived from the gully above it (Plate 22B). A sparse growth of vegetation has become established in the finer-grained rock material of the upper part of the cone.

Rock debris on the surrounding slopes of Blue Mountain shows the same kind of irregular horizontal striping you saw in the soil ripples farther down the trail. This is yet another expression of the effects of interaction between gravity and freeze-thaw cycles.

The jagged, frost-shattered ridge on the Continental Divide north of Blue Mountain contrasts sharply with glacially smoothed rock below.

Stop 8: *Independence Lake basin*

Two features often found at the heads of glaciated valleys are cirques and tarns. Cirques have the same general shape as spring bowls, but a different origin. At the onset of a glacial episode, snow begins to accumulate on the leeward sides of ridges in permanent snowbanks, called *firn*. In summer, meltwater from a firn bank percolates down through the snow, saturating the ground and the bedrock beneath it. The following winter, this water freezes and expands, shattering the surface of the bedrock. Since firn flows slowly downhill, this shattered rock debris is gradually scoured away, leaving a bowl-shaped depression. This process has been called *nivation*.

As average annual temperatures drop, more snow accumulates in winter than melts in summer. The firn bank thickens, and its already dense snow becomes further compacted into glacial ice. At this point, the scouring and abrading action of rock material caught between the ice and the bedrock becomes an even more effective mechanism for deepening and widening the cirque than nivation.

Tarns are glacial lakes, like Independence, sitting in the bottoms of cirques (Plate 22A). They are simply the most depressed parts of cirque floors. To the east of Independence Lake is another, smaller tarn (Plate 22B), whose east bank is formed by the steep front of a rock glacier (see Plate 21A). Rock glaciers are similar in form and behavior to ice glaciers, but while the latter are mostly ice with a few rounded boulders, rock glaciers are mostly angular boulders with a little ice, enough to maintain a slow downhill flow.

Notice the difference in appearance between the rock glacier, with its steep front and lobate form, and the large rockslide to the north of the lake.

From the smaller tarn, walk northwest around the north end of Independence Lake, then up toward the trail that climbs to the pass northwest of the lake.

Stop 9: *Geissler Pass*

This pass separates the glacial cirque of Independence Lake from that of Lostman Lake. The glaciated valley of Lostman Creek extends to the west, eventually joining the Roaring Fork River at Lostman Campground. Beyond the sharp ridge that forms the north wall of Lostman Creek Valley, another glaciated valley, that of the North Fork of the Fryingpan River, extends to the north, joining the Roaring Fork at Basalt.

The peak rising from the west end of the pass is North Geissler Mountain. Glacial erosion and nivation on all sides of it, but most particularly on the northeast, have carved it into a rather steep, pyramidal shape called a *horn*, a German term for the same feature in the Swiss and Austrian Alps.

Underfoot, the rocky soil of the pass exhibits fairly well developed *polygonal ground* (Plate 23A). Frost polygons, measuring about two or three feet across, are formed by seasonal freeze and thaw gradually pushing the larger rock fragments away from rather evenly spaced freezing centers. These large fragments eventually collect in a coarse, "chicken wire" network with fine-grained, moss-covered soil in the "holes."

The bedrock of the pass is quartz monzonite (3), a granitic rock that was intruded into the biotite gneiss (1) 1.47 billion years ago. Its inferior resistance to erosion, in comparison with the gneiss, is the most logical explanation for the location of the pass at this point.

From here, go back down the same trail, but stay to the west (right) of Independence Lake, continuing south on the alp (the flattish bench between the valley and the ridge to the west). The trail is obscure and intermittent. Don't worry if you lose it; just follow the alp to its far end. The swales, or depressions, in the otherwise flat surface are caused by the slow downhill creep of water-saturated soil.

When you come to the edge of the large springbowl, you will have to contour around it to the right (west) to avoid losing altitude and then having to regain it. Wildflowers are especially abundant here.

Stop 10: *Small ponds*

These are *kettle ponds,* formed by the melting of large blocks of ice embedded in glacial ground moraine. Notice that just northwest of these ponds the planed bedrock surface of the alp gives way to glacial moraine that has been built up to the same level as the planed bedrock. The remainder of the alp is all in moraine.

Above you, on the skyline ridge to the northwest, you may see a long snow cornice left over from the winter where high winds blew snow over the ridge to accumulate in a thick, dense deposit of firn on the lee side.

Follow the alp to its south end and walk down the steep, springy hillside to a small lake below.

Stop 11: *Linkins Lake*

This is another tarn lake in a glacial cirque. The glacier that lay in this short valley was a lot smaller than the one that flowed down the Roaring Fork Valley, to which it was a tributary. Because the Roaring Fork's glacier deepened its valley considerably more than the Linkins glacier did, the Linkins Valley therefore enters that of the Roaring Fork high up on the valley wall. This is known as a *hanging valley* relationship.

There is another small kettle pond, now filled with silt and boulders of schist, just north of Linkins Lake. It supports an abundant growth of sedges. On the slope to the north of the kettle pond is a small mine adit (tunnel) with a dump below it.

Walk south-east along the lakeshore until you come to the outlet stream. Then follow this to where it drops over the lip of the hanging valley in a deep V-notch gorge.

Since the last glaciation, the stream has cut down through the unconsolidated glacial moraine of the steep sidewall of the Roaring Fork Valley. Many processes are at work to reduce the steepness of the valley sideslopes resulting from the passage of glaciers. This streamcut is one; soil creep and landslides are others. If no further glaciations were to occur here (a very unlikely possibility), the characteristic U-shape of the glaciated valleys would gradually be lost as these processes would slowly remove material from the steeper, higher regions and deposit it on the lower parts of the slopes.

Walk north from here (left as you look across the Roaring Fork Valley) into a gentle swale, on the far side of which you will encounter a trail leading down by switchbacks toward the Roaring Fork River.

Stop 12: *Trail crosses a small, but prominent ridge*

This is a *lateral moraine,* a ridge of rock debris left between the valley sidewall and the edge of the glacier.

Hunter Creek Trail (lower part)

¼ day; 1½ miles; elevation gain 480 feet from the trailhead at 7870 feet to top of steep section at junction with upper branch of Hunter Creek trail at 8350 feet.

USGS Topographic Quadrangle Map: Aspen
USGS Geologic Quadrangle Map: Aspen GQ-933.

Access: From the Jerome Hotel, Main and Mill streets, Aspen, drive north on Mill Street and cross the bridge over the Roaring Fork River, then bear left up the hill and turn right at the hospital. From here, a silver sign marking the trailhead is visible just to the left of the Silverking Apartments.

Stop 1: *Trailhead*

The ground that the Silverking Apartment complex is on is earth fill from a recent ore milling operation. Above and behind the trailhead sign, Hunter Creek has cut its channel down through landslide deposits derived from the steep west slope of Smuggler Mountain to the east of you. Most of that slope is composed of glacial moraine (30) of the Second Valley glaciation. Since the Second Valley, two subsequent glaciers have descended the Roaring Fork gorge, the Third and Youngest Valley, but these were less extensive than the Second Valley, and their moraines did not extend beyond the east edge of Aspen. The large, rounded boulders in the streambed came from the moraine, in which they were haphazardly intermingled with cobbles, gravel, sand, silt, and clay.

Stop 2: *First bridge crossing a dry channel*

This is a flood channel of Hunter Creek. Floods on montane streams are of two kinds: high snowmelt runoff in spring, and cloudburst floods in summer. Usually, snowmelt floods rise slowly, and do little damage. Cloudburst floods, on the other hand, rise very quickly, and even though they typically have a smaller rate of flow than snowmelt floods, their destructive impact is much greater.

The lower reach of Hunter Creek has a special flood problem because of the fairly recent landslide deposits that have been dumped into the valley. Each time a large cloudburst flood occurs, these deposits are shifted around, and new flood channels are formed, like this one. Eventually, enough of the landslide material will be washed down into the Roaring Fork that Hunter Creek will again be able to maintain a single stable channel capable of containing large floods.

Notice the natural levee of boulders that lines the south side of the flood channel.

Stop 3: *First clearing; boulder levee to the left*

This large boulder levee from a more recent flood has cut off the dry channel you crossed at the first bridge. That channel is now on your right. Notice the stand of scarred aspens on the left that have been partially buried by the boulder levee. Hunter Creek flows in the channel beyond the levee, with red sandy siltstone of the Maroon Formation (12) forming the opposite bank. The Maroon Formation was originally laid down, about 293 to 270 million years ago, as flood deposits derived from two high ranges of the Ancestral Rocky Mountains to the east and southwest of Aspen. Its strata, originally nearly horizontal, have been tilted upward through a 55-degree angle during the rise of the Sawatch Range east of Aspen about 72 million years ago. Uplift of the Sawatch Range and the surrounding region has continued intermittently since then.

Stop 4: *Just beyond clearing*

The growth of lichens on these boulders indicates that they have been undisturbed by floods for a while. In contrast, the boulders in the flood levees you saw are nearly bare of lichens.

Stop 5: *Second bridge*

This is another flood channel in landslide debris.

Stop 6: *Trail drops down a short, steep bank to a stream crossing*

Here, the surface of the landslide fan has been cut by Hunter Creek, forming this steep bank. The aspen meadow to the right is on the fan surface. Just around the bend in the trail are several large aspens partially buried in flood-transported boulders. The presence of lichens on these boulders indicates that the flooding was not very recent.

Stop 7: *First large bridge across Hunter Creek*

The large boulders in the creek bed are mostly composed of biotite gneiss (1), at 1.7 billion years, the oldest rock type in the Aspen area. This rock unit is widely exposed east of Aspen in the Sawatch Range. These boulders were torn from bedrock by mountain glaciers, smoothed and rounded in transport, and finally deposited as Second Valley glacial moraine (30). A long terrace remnant of this moraine has escaped erosion on the southwest sides of Red and Smuggler mountains. The landslide mentioned earlier brought these boulders to their present position in the creek bed. Most of them are too large to be moved by even the most powerful floods on Hunter Creek.

The other side of the landslide fan surface is at the west end of the footbridge.

Stop 8: *Second bridge across Hunter Creek*

The ground approaching the bridge is in Second Valley glacial moraine (30). Notice the huge rounded boulders mixed with finer material including gravel, sand, silt, and clay.

Stop 9: *Third bridge across Hunter Creek*

The irregular, bouldery land surface at the east end of the bridge is in debris from a rather recent landslide. From across the bridge you can see the landslide scar in glacial moraine on the west face of Smuggler Mountain (Plate 23B).

Stop 10: *Large boulder slope on left*

These large moraine boulders were moved first by a Second Valley glacier and then by road machinery. On the largest boulder, a sharp line separates a lichen-covered area from bare rock. The bare portion, of course, was buried before the boulder was moved.

Shortly above this point, the Hunter Creek Trail is joined by a branch trail from the left, whereupon it crosses another bridge over Hunter Creek, and proceeds upward into a broad, formerly glaciated valley with aspen groves and wildflower meadows (Plates 24A and B, and cover photograph). The scenery in this valley is beautiful, but we have chosen to end the trail log here because of the lack of definite landmarks by which to identify specific stops along the trail.

Grizzly Lake Trail

1 day, 6 miles; elevation gain 1945 feet from the trailhead at 10,575 feet to Grizzly Lake at 12,520 feet.

USGS Topographic Quadrangle Map: Independence Pass.

Access: Follow the access directions for the Lincoln Creek Road. From the Grizzly Reservoir outlet at the end of that log, a road continues left up a hill, and then drops abruptly into the Portal Campground. The trailhead is at the crest of the hill, on the left, marked by a Forest Service sign designating the types of travel permitted on the trail.

Stop 1: *Trailhead*

The rock type that makes up the peaks and ridges around you is a 34-million-year-old quartz latite porphyry related to the White Rock Granodiorite (22), which underlies most of the country to the southwest of Aspen. This is an igneous rock, similar to granite, which rose through the Earth's crust as a body of molten magma. As the rising magma approached the land surface, great volumes of lava were erupted over the landscape to form the rock unit known as the Grizzly Andesite (23). You will see outcrops of this unit higher up on the Grizzly Lake Trail. After the eruptions, a large area of ground, about nine miles in diameter, fractured and settled into the magma chamber below. You are standing a little north of the center of this feature, which is technically known as a *collapse caldera*.

Following the eruption of lava, the caldera entered an explosive phase during which dense clouds of white hot ash were blown high into the atmosphere. With each explosion, these glowing clouds then avalanched over the countryside, still hot enough to weld themselves into a hard, dense rock called ash-flow tuff. This deposit is quite widespread in the Grizzly caldera area; you will encounter it, too, farther up the trail.

On the slope north of you are several prominent snow avalanche courses. Mature spruce-fir forest borders these chutes, but little vegetation grows within them. The lower ends of the chutes are filled with rockslide debris, or talus.

Stop 2: *About 100 yards up trail, in forest*

To the right of the trail is a steep ravine. This has been cut by Grizzly Creek since the latest glaciation, which probably ended about 10,000 years ago. While the glaciers were still in these valleys, they scoured out their walls and floors into broad, U-shaped troughs, deepening the valleys to varying degrees. Larger valleys, filled by larger glaciers, were deepened more than smaller valleys were. Consequently, small valleys, like that of Grizzly Creek, were generally left entering large ones, like that of Lincoln Creek, at a higher elevation. This circumstance is called a *hanging valley* relationship, and Grizzly Creek is in one such hanging valley. The creek is cutting down through the soft glacial moraine at the valley mouth in an attempt to reestablish a smooth gradient from its headwaters to its junction with Lincoln Creek.

Stop 3: *First clearing*

This gentle meadow at the top of the steep hill you have just climbed is the floor of the glacial valley of Grizzly Creek. To your right is the ravine, where the creek is cutting down through both glacial moraine and bedrock.

Stop 4: *About 100 yards into the clearing*

You are standing in an avalanche path, one of many that keep this valley partially cleared of forest trees, thereby providing a habitat for many annual summer wildflowers, which are especially varied and abundant in this valley.

Mature spruce-fir forest flanks the avalanche track. In its lower course, aspen and willow grow upon rockslide debris, which extends below the trail for some distance. Notice the hummocky topography and the angular, lichen-covered blocks of the slide debris. On the right edge of the trail is a mature Engelmann spruce that has been scarred and broken by both rockfall and snow avalanches.

On the other side of the valley, best seen from a bit farther up the trail, is another large avalanche path. Recent rockslide activity in this path is indicated by a sinuous trench with little or no vegetation, extending down the talus fan at the base of the chute. A meander bend of Grizzly Creek has cut the toe of the fan on its eastern side.

Stop 5: *Angular rock fragments in trail*

This material is rockslide debris, or talus, derived from the steep, narrow avalanche gully to the north. The talus has been largely overgrown by herbaceous vegetation since it slid into its present position.

A bit farther on, on the right side of the trail, is an Englemann spruce showing a typical "avalanche flag" growth form. The crown has been snapped off, together with the branches on the uphill side. On the downhill side, however, and at the base, the foliage is very dense where it is protected from avalanche damage.

Stop 6: *Trail reenters forest*

The presence of the large trees here indicates that this area is free of major snow avalanches.

Stop 7: *Trail crosses a dry, rocky channel*

This is a flood trench in an alluvial fan. Various processes are at work on the glacially oversteepened walls of the valley to restore the original gentler slope profile that was present before glaciation. Where gravity is the main moving force, the result is a rockslide. Where both gravity and water act on movable slope material, the result is either a landslide or a mudflow, depending on the amount of water present. Mudflow deposits usually form fanshaped deposits, appropriately called alluvial fans. This one has been deeply cut by an unusually heavy flood, probably resulting from a summer cloudburst.

The rocks in the flood trench are all fresh, without a covering of lichen, and with only a few annual herbs. These observations suggest that the trench was cut quite recently. The exact year in which it was cut could probably be determined by taking tree ring cores from the three large, dead Englemann spruce on the channel bank uphill to your right. These trees would have stopped producing annual growth rings when their root systems were exposed by the channel cutting. Tree ring cross-dating with other live spruces nearby would reveal the age of the youngest ring in the dead spruce if the relative year-to-year ring widths are variable enough to form a distinctive pattern that can be matched among different trees. This variability in ring width is largely controlled by climatic factors, especially the depth of winter snowpack, and it has been used extensively in the dating of archaeological materials.

Attempts are being made to reconstruct past climatic

behavior with the use of tree rings, but such attempts are limited by the fact that ring growth is controlled by many factors other than the ones most often chosen for analysis: average monthly precipitation and temperature. For example, a freak cold snap and snowstorm occurred in mid-June, 1976, in the Rocky Mountains. In Aspen, it killed most of the new growth on spruces, Douglas-firs, subalpine fir, Gambel oak and many other perennial species. This suppressed annual growth severely for 1976 and probably for one or more years afterward. The narrow rings for these years would then be interpreted, by the methods now in use, as indicative of prolonged drought!

The cobbles and boulders in this channel are composed of quartz latite porphyry. Several of them have darker inclusions of biotite gneiss (1), the older country rock into which the quartz latite magma was intruded.

Stop 8: *Meadow with snowfields often forming a bridge across Grizzly Creek*

This feature may not be here every year. It depends on the activity of the snow avalanche chutes above you on both sides of the valley. When we came through in 1976, the deposit of avalanche snow was extensive, and the outlines of large, angular blocks of snow were clearly visible within the snowfields. This kind of blocky deposit is from hard slab avalanches in which the sliding snow is cohesive enough to maintain its structure. In loose snow avalanches, on the other hand, the snow cover slides as an incoherent mass of rolling, turbulent powder.

Beneath the avalanche paths are landslide fans whose bases coalesce in the bottom of the valley. The creek has cut its channel down through the fan material; probably there was a small pond here before it did so.

Stop 9: *Open slope with two parallel trails just beyond a spruce/fir grove; avalanche-damaged and stunted Englemann spruce are scattered over this slope*

Stop 10: *Rather copious spring on right*

This is a springbowl. Water-saturated earth material flows quite easily downslope, so where springs emerge on hillsides, frequently they are located in bowl-shaped depressions like this from which the earth has gradually been washed away.

Stop 11: *Rockslide cones on left valley wall*

The degree to which these talus cones are vegetated is a good index of how active they are. Vegetation will gradually cover and stabilize an inactive cone that is receiving no additional talus from above.

Stop 12: *Stream crossing*

Here is a good place from which to see the typical U-shape of the cross profile of a glaciated valley. That shape has been more or less extensively modified by rockslide, landslide and mudflow activity on the valley sideslopes.

Stop 13: *About 100 feet beyond the stream crossing*

On the opposite valley wall, a bit farther on, is a talus cone with a sinuous rockslide channel running down its surface. Notice the conspicuous levees of rock debris that have formed on the edges of the channel.

Stop 14: *Trail crosses a small tributary stream*

The Continental Divide ridge on the opposite side of the valley is composed of andesite lava flows (23) from the earlier, nonexplosive phase of the Grizzly caldera. The individual lava flow sheets are clearly outlined by alternating bands of cliffs and talus.

The rusty color of the boulders in the bed of Grizzly Creek is caused by iron oxide derived from the weathering of pyrite (iron disulfide) in mineralized rock farther upvalley.

Stop 15: *Top of steep section; flattish meadow*

You are on an alp. Alps are not high, snowy peaks, but gentle meadows on the shoulders of high, snowy peaks. They are the remnants of old high valley floors below which mountain valley glaciers have carved deep, narrow, U-shaped canyons. The abundance of these old valley floor remnants in the European Alps gave those mountains their name.

During the winter, a prominent snow cornice develops on the skyline ridge to the left. This may persist well into the summer. To the left of the cornice is Grizzly Peak, 13,988 feet high and largely hidden by a substantial pinnacle in the foreground, around which two strands of the Grizzly glacier flowed from the glacial cirque above.

To your right is a *kettle pond*, formed by the melting of a large block of ice that was embedded in glacial moraine.

Stop 16: *Cairn (rock pile) in trail*

Turn left at this marker, and follow similar ones to the top of the next rise. Then continue in the same general direction toward a trail that rises at an angle, eastward toward Grizzly Peak, up a prominent talus slope beyond the meadow.

The flattish surface here is probably another higher alp. A large kettle pond is present near the base of the talus slope. The rock outcrops of Grizzly Andesite lava here have been severely shattered by frost action, forming a Felsenmeer, a German term meaning "sea of rock." Where the rocks are less shattered, they show evidence of glacial scour.

Stop 17: *First rock outcrop on talus slope*

Limonite, a hydrous oxide of iron, gives this andesite outcrop its rusty color. Limonite is a weathering product of various iron-bearing sulfide minerals which may also contain precious or base metals, that is, gold and silver or copper, lead, and zinc. These sulfide ores are usually emplaced by hot water solutions emanating from subterranean magma chambers. The ore minerals are deposited as veins in cracks developed in the country rock. When erosion exposes these veins to the atmosphere, they become weathered, and the metal sulfides are altered to metal oxides, while the sulfur is released as sulfuric acid and metal sulfates. Prospectors use this kind of rusty iron stain in rocks as a guide to ore mineral deposits. Study of the form of the limonite in weathered outcrops can actually reveal the parent mineral from which the limonite was derived, thereby indicating whether the deposit merits further exploration.

Stop 18: *Crest of trail at Grizzly Lake outlet*

One branch of the Grizzly glacier flowed out over this lip. The rather narrow notch here may have been caused by a later, minor glaciation during the Little Ice Age, a worldwide cold spell during the 17th to 19th centuries, A.D.

The odd, small washout to the right of the trail is hard to explain. Perhaps a spring formerly emerged here, but has since dried up.

Stop 19: *Grizzly Lake*

This is a *glacial tarn*, a small lake filling a rock basin scooped out by a glacier in the floor of the cirque in which it originated. On the south side of the lake, a *protalus rampart* has developed where rock debris has rolled down the permanent snowfield to accumulate on its downhill edge at the lakeshore. Large talus cones surround other portions of the lake. That these, and the rampart, are actively accumulating new talus is shown by the slump scars at their bases where they enter the lake. To your left is the lake outlet, located in the outlet passage of the other branch of the Grizzly glacier.

Grizzly Peak is composed of three rock units. Its western part is 34-million-year-old quartz latite porphyry (22), the eastern slopes are slightly younger, explosive Grizzly Ash-flow Tuff (24) and the Grizzly Lake basin is Grizzly Andesite lava (23) of intermediate age.

Independence Pass Road and Ute Trail

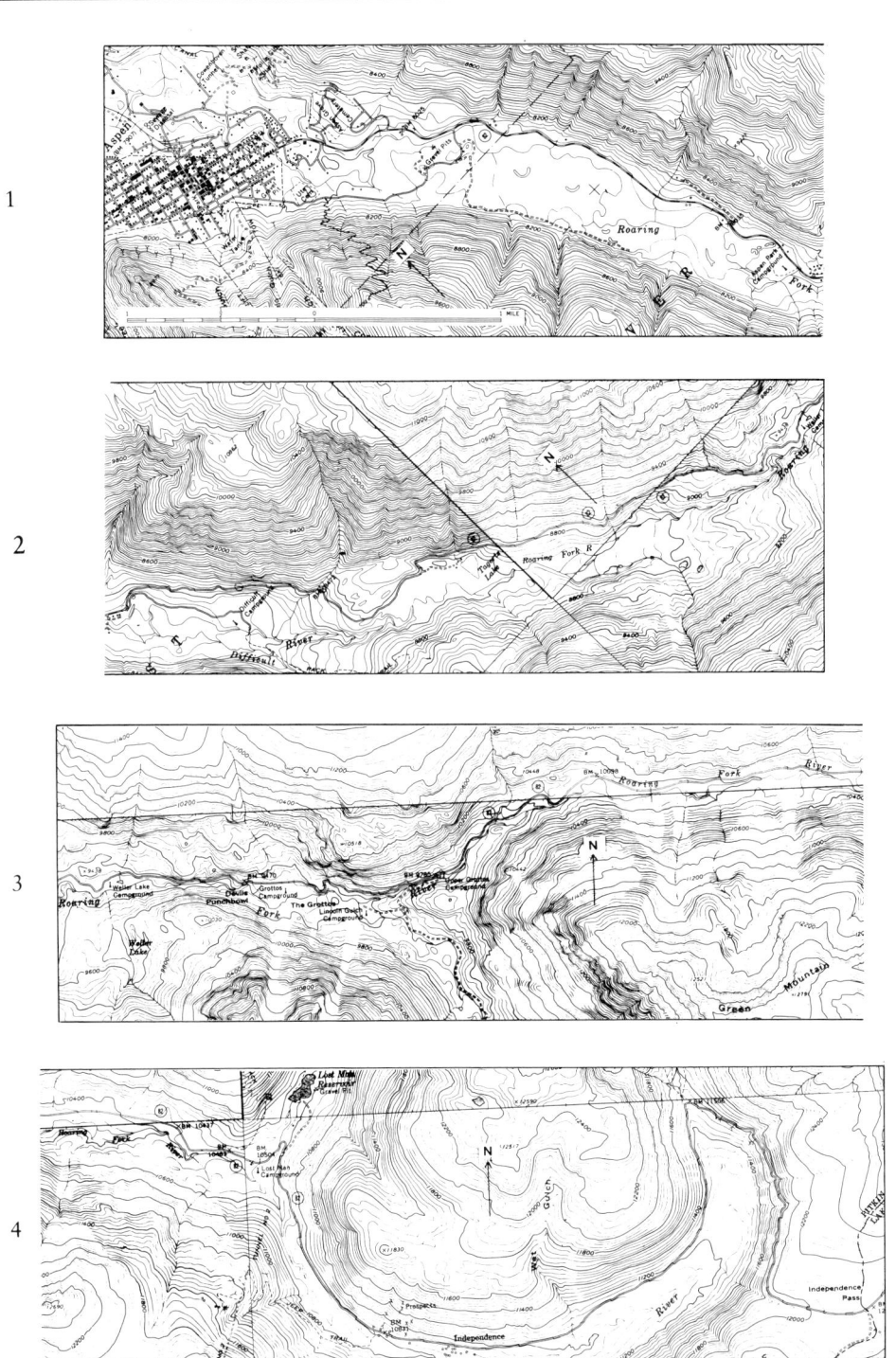

Castle Creek Road

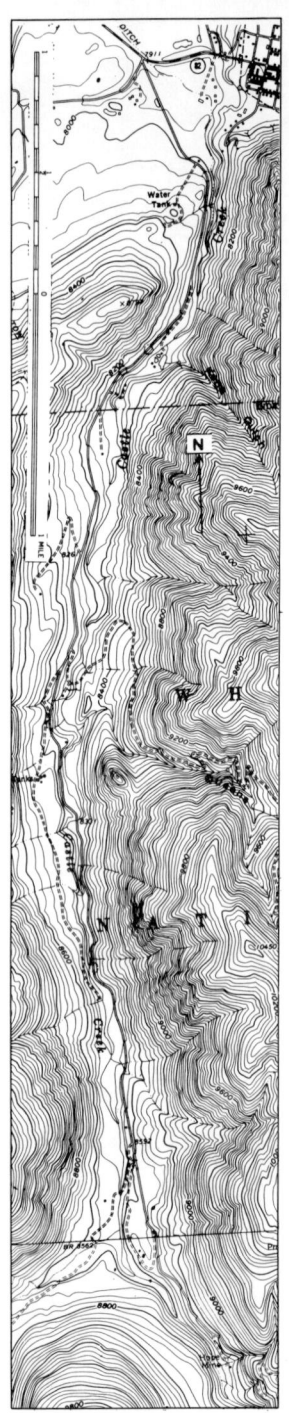
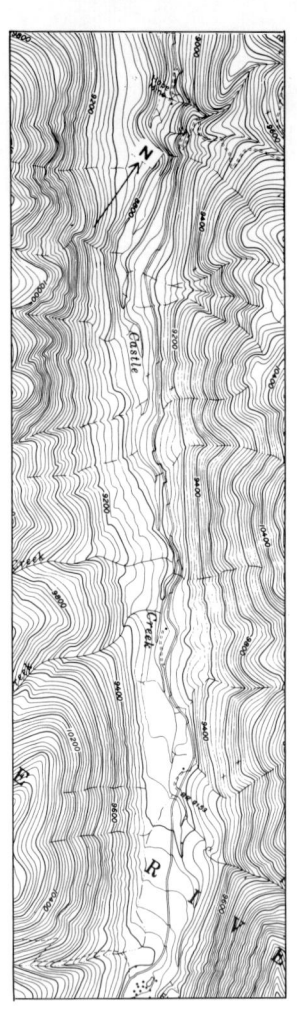
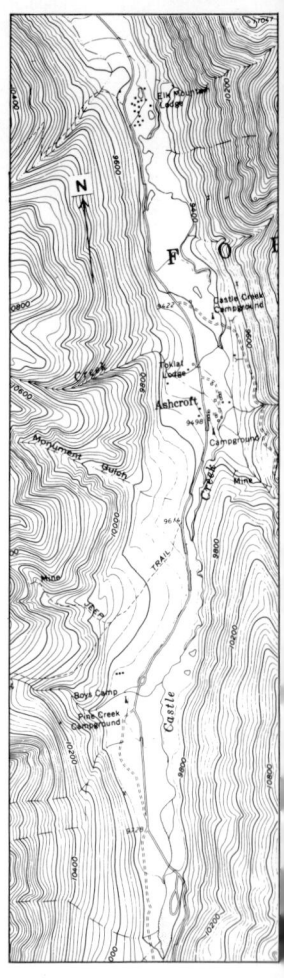

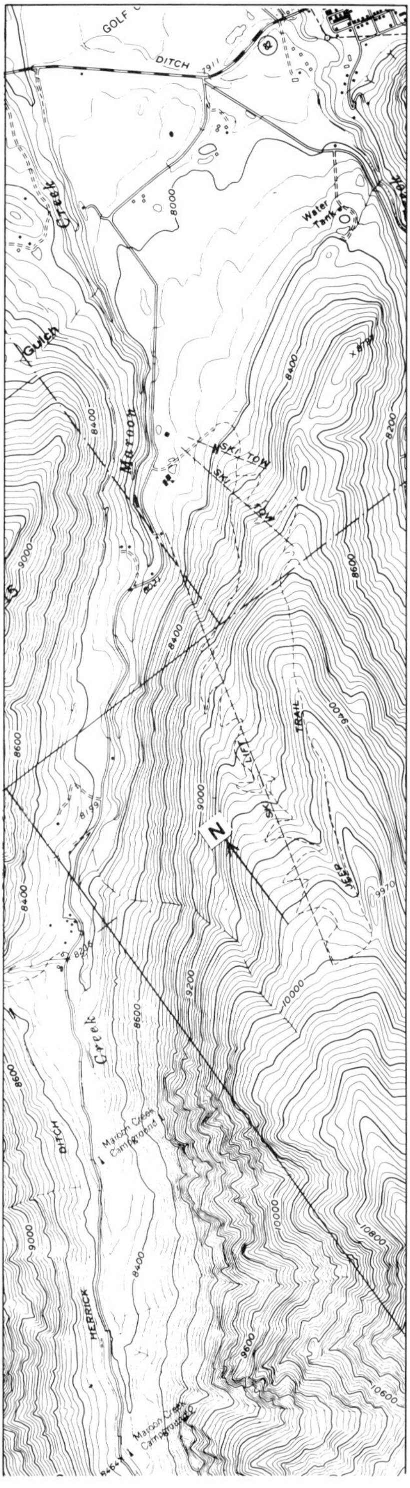
GOLF
DITCH
7911
82
Creek
Water Tank
8000
Gulch
8400
Maroon
8200
SKI TOW
9000
8600
TRAIL
9400
SKI LIFT
N
JEEP
9970
9200
10000
Creek
Maroon Creek Campground
DITCH
HERRICK
10800
9600
10600

1

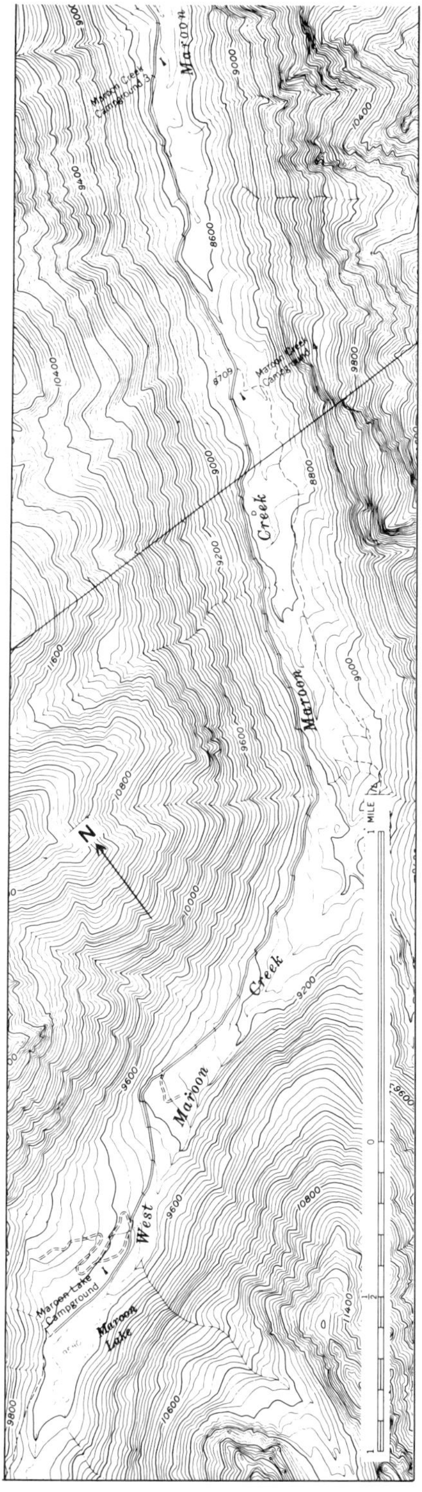
Maroon
Maroon Creek Campground
9000
10400
9400
8600
9800
Maroon Creek Campground
8800
Creek
9200
11600
Maroon
10800
N
MILE
10000
Creek
Maroon
West
9600
Maroon Lake Campground
Maroon Lake
11400
10600

2

Lincoln Creek Road

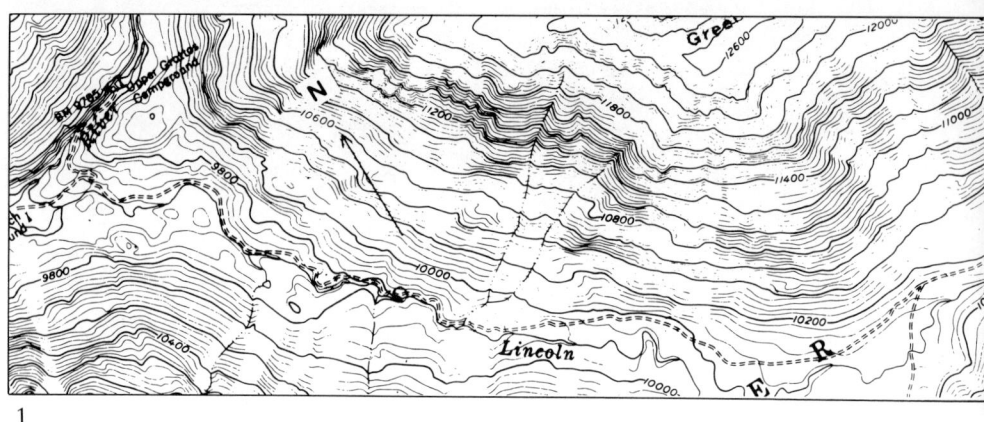

1

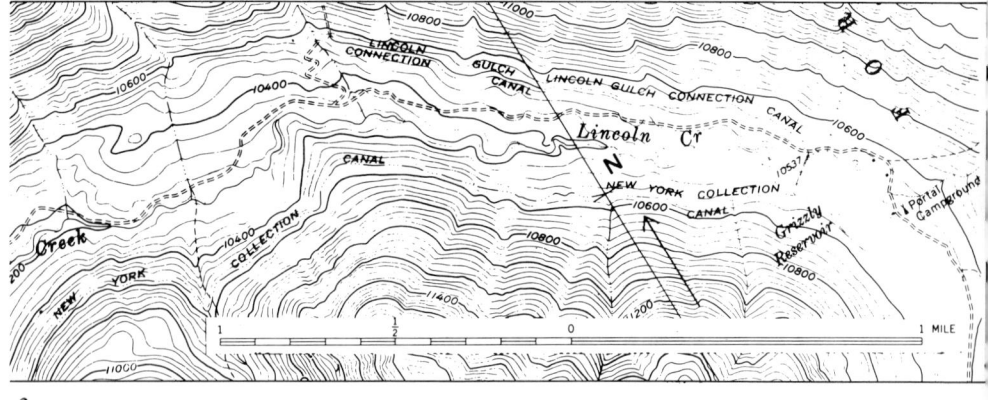

2

Woody Creek Road and Rio Grande Trail

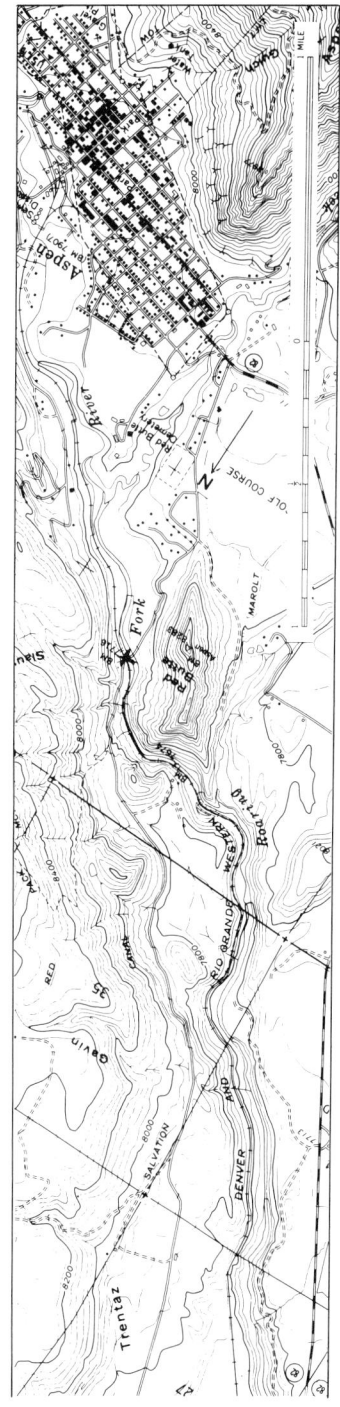

1

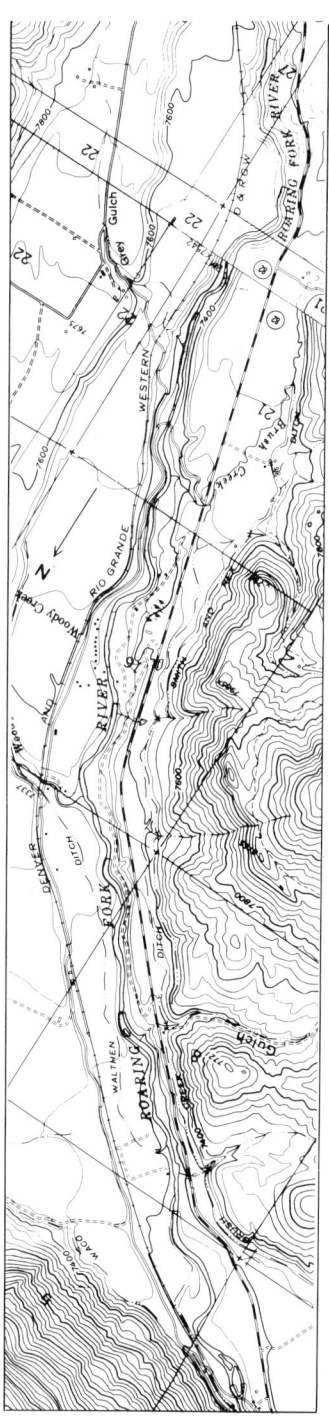

2

Grizzly Lake, Buckskin Pass, Independence Lake, and Hunter Creek Trails

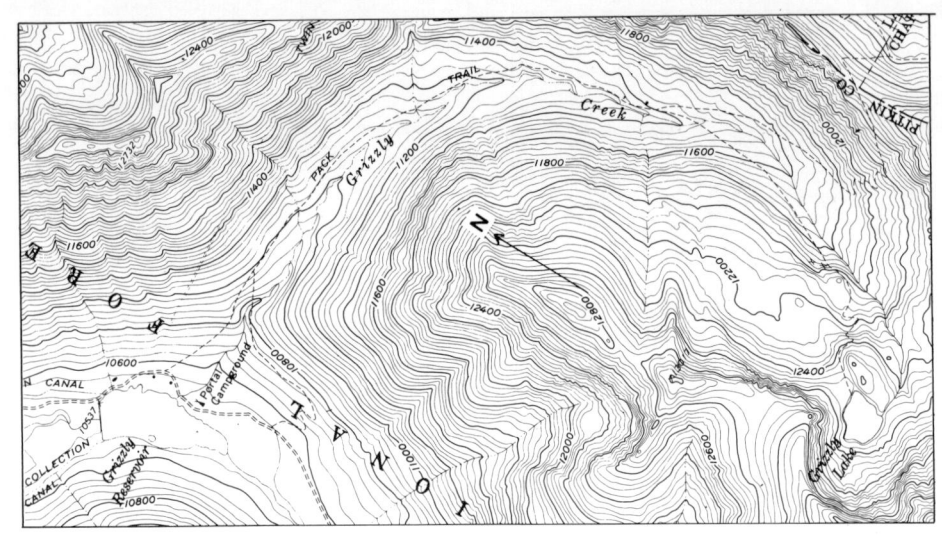
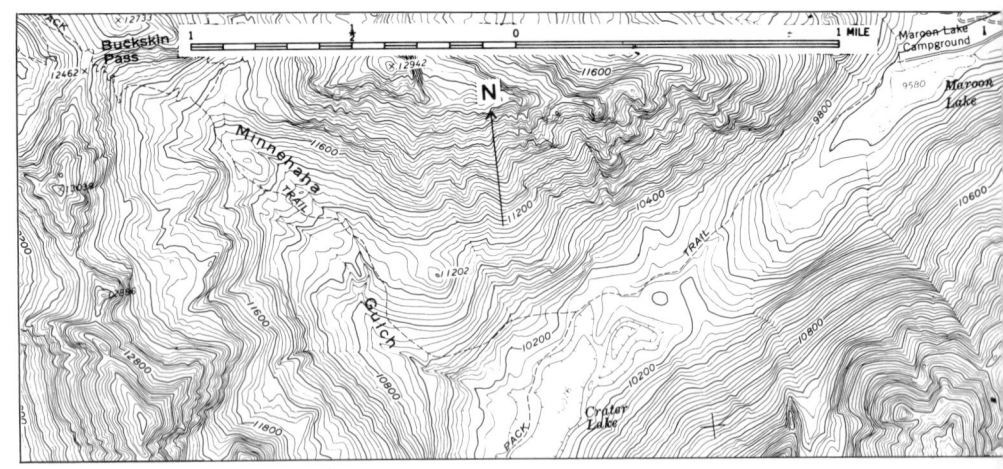
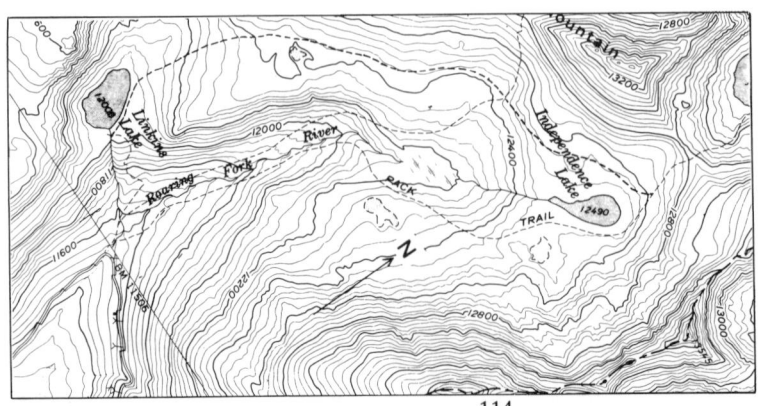
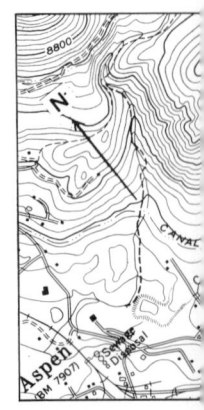

Glossary

A

ablation: melting and evaporation of glacial ice or snow.

adit: a horizontal mine entrance tunnel.

alluvial: deposited by rivers.

alp: a terrace remnant of a valley floor below which a deeper valley has been cut, usually by glacial *erosion*.

amphibole: a group of complex, hydrous silicates of iron, aluminum, calcium, magnesium, and sodium, of which the commonest is hornblende: $(Ca, Na)_3(Mg, Fe^{++}, Al, Ti)_5(Si, Al)_8 O_{22}(OH, F)_2$, a shiny, black mineral with perfect prismatic *cleavage* with cleavage angles of 56 and 124 degrees.

Ancestral Front Range: a high mountain range passing north-northwest through central Colorado about 313 to 270 million years ago, with its axis slightly west of the axis of the modern Front Range.

Ancestral Rocky Mountains: the *Ancestral Front* and *Uncompahgre Ranges*.

Ancestral Uncompahgre Range: a high mountain range, curving northwest across the southwest quadrant of Colorado about 300 to 270 million years ago.

andesite: a fine-grained, often *porphyritic, extrusive igneous* rock intermediate in composition between *granite* and *basalt*. Essential minerals are sodic *plagioclase, proxene,* and *biotite.*

anticline: a fold in *stratified* rocks with older strata toward the inside; usually ridgelike in form.

aplite: a fine-grained *intrusive* rock of *granitic* composition and texture.

argillite: a weakly-metamorphosed, highly *indurated shale, mudstone,* or *siltstone.*

ash-flow tuff: dense, fine-grained rock of *granitic* to *andesitic* composition formed by the hot-welding of fragments of *volcanic ash* and glass as they fall to the ground from the eruption cloud.

B

basal glide plane: the surface of contact between a large, coherent *landslide* block and the ground over which it has slid.

basalt: a black, fine-grained *extrusive* rock, the principal substance of the Earth's *crust* (and possibly also the *mantle* as denser, but chemically equivalent eclogite), mainly exposed in the ocean basins.

base elevation: the height above sea level of the base of the mountains.

base level: the lower limit of potential stream *erosion* in a given region.

batholith: a body of *intrusive igneous* rock of non-tabular form and measuring more than 40 square miles in its largest horizontal extent.

bedding plane: a surface between two depositional layers within a sediment or *sedimentary* rock.

biotite: a dark brown to black mica; composition $K(Mg, Fe^{++})_3 (Al, Fe^{+++} Si_3O)_{10}(OH)_2$; perfect basal *cleavage*, forming thin sheets.

broad valley surface: a system of shallow valleys cut about 1000 feet below the *Rocky Mountain erosion surface* between about 10 and 8 million years ago; now largely destroyed by more recent, deeper canyon cutting.

C

calcite: calcium carbonate, $CaCO_3$; crystalline, colorless, and transparent when pure, with perfect, rhombohedral *cleavage*.

calcareous: containing *calcite*.

caldera: a large, roughly circular area at the Earth's surface above an *igneous magma* chamber where the *country rock* has either collapsed into the chamber, been blown away from the chamber, or both.

carbonaceous: containing carbon, usually of organic derivation.

carbonate: any compound containing the carbonate radical, $CO_3^=$; especially *calcite* $CaCO_3$, and *dolomite*, $CaMg(CO_3)_2$.

Castle Creek fault zone: a linear zone of faulting, bordering the Sawatch Range on the west in the Castle Creek valley south of Aspen, and following the Roaring Fork valley between Aspen and Basalt.

Central Colorado Trough: a broad, shallow-marine depression between the *Ancestral Front* and *Uncompahgre ranges*.

chert: massive, minutely crystalline *silica* formed in *sedimentary* rocks by reprecipitation of dissolved *siliceous* animal and plant skeletons and *volcanic ash*.

chrysocolla: hydrous copper silicate, $CuSiO_3 \bullet 2H_2O$; no *cleavage;* resembles turquoise, but adheres to the tongue, unlike turquoise.

cirque: a topographic bowl formed at or above permanent snowline by a *firn* bank or glacier.

clastic: literally, "broken"; composed of rock fragments; clastic rocks include *conglomerate, sandstone,* and *shale*.

claystone: *indurated* clay; grain size less than 1/256mm.

cleavage: the tendency of a mineral or rock to split in preferred plane directions. *Cubic cleavage* produces rectangular, blocky forms; *octahedral cleavage* makes pyramids and equilateral triangles; *rhombohedral cleavage* gives diamond shapes; *prismatic cleavage* yields bladed forms; *pinacoidal cleavage* results in various flat forms including thin, flaky ones, produced by a special form of pinacoidal cleavage known as *basal cleavage*.

Colorado Mineral Belt: a zone of mineral deposition extending from northeast Arizona to Boulder, Colorado, formed about 72 to 53 million years ago.

Colorado Plateau: a high, stable region of the Earth's *crust* to the west of the Rocky Mountains and east of the *Great Basin*.

compressive stress: a squeezing force.

confluence: the junction of two rivers.

conglomerate: a very coarse *clastic* rock composed of gravel to boulder-sized particles in a *matrix* of finer-grained cementing material.

contact: a surface between two distinct *rock units*.

continental drift: the slow rafting of continents across the Earth's surface upon *basaltic* plates that grow laterally upon one edge at *spreading rifts*.

Cordilleran geosyncline: a belt of thick sediment accumulation that existed at the western edge of the North American continent between about 800 and 150 million years ago before being uplifted, metamorphosed, and welded onto the continent as the *Western Cordillera*.

cornice: a thick, often overhanging deposit of dense snow, or *firn*, that forms on the leeward side of a steep, exposed ridge.

country rock: the rock into which an *igneous intrusion* is emplaced.

crag: a rugged cliff.

Cretaceous seaway: a broad, shallow marine depression that existed in central North America between the Arctic Ocean and the Gulf of Mexico about 105-65 million years ago.

crossbedding: *bedding planes* that lie at various angles to the planar surfaces that outline a *rock unit*. These are caused by wind or running water.

cross-profile: the shape of a valley across its long axis.

crust: the outer, brittle shell of the Earth, varying in thickness between 5 and 23 miles.

crystalline: composed of interlocking mineral crystals.

D

dike: a tabular body of *intrusive igneous* rock that does not lie parallel to *bedding* or *foliation planes* in the *country rock*.

dolomite: calcium magnesium carbonate, $CaMg(CO_3)_2$; colorless and transparent when pure, with perfect *rhombohedral cleavage*; both a mineral species and monomineralic rock type.

drag fold: a minor fold that reflects the major geologic structure and forces that have affected a region.

E

East Pacific Rise: a major *spreading rift* forming the boundary between the northwestward moving *Pacific plate* and the eastward moving *Farallon plate*. The Rise has been largely *subducted* beneath the western margin of North America.

ecology: the study of the relationships of organisms to their physical environments (autecology) and the inter-relationships among organisms (synecology).

epicontinental sea: a shallow sea on a continental surface.

erosion: the chemical and mechanical breakdown, and especially the subsequent transport by gravity, wind, water or ice, of surficial bedrock material.

erosion surface: a nearly flat surface produced by long-continued *erosion*.

extrusive: *igneous* material poured out on the Earth's surface.

F

fan: a very low, flat, half-conical deposit of loose rock or earth material formed at a break in a topographic slope.

Farallon plate: a *basaltic* crustal plate whose western edge is formed by the **East Pacific Rise**. This plate has been largely *subducted* beneath the west coast of North America.

fault: a break in the Earth's crust along which movement has taken place.

feldspar: orthoclase: potassium aluminum silicate, $KAlSi_3O_8$, and plagioclase, including albite: sodium aluminum silicate, $NaAlSi_3O_8$, and anorthite: calcium aluminum silicate, $CaAl_2Si_2O_8$. Orthoclase is white to pink; albite is usually white, and anorthite varies from white to gray. Most plagioclase is a hybrid between albite and anorthite. Both orthoclase and plagioclase have good basal and side pinacoidal *cleavage*, with a cleavage angle of 90 degrees in orthoclase, and about 94 degrees in plagioclase.

Felsenmeer: an extensive deposit of frost-shattered, jagged rock on mountain summits and high ridges.

firn: dense, compacted snow with a density between .4 and .8.

flint: see *chert*.

float: pieces of rock that have become detached from their parent *rock unit*.

floodplain: a flat-topped deposit of mud, sand and/or gravel deposited above and adjacent to the channel banks by a river in flood stage.

foliation plane: a plane in *igneous* or *metamorphic* rock along which platy minerals are aligned.

formation: a *rock unit* including all *strata* or other deposits that logically appear to belong together by virtue of rock type or mode of origin.

frost polygon: a ring of large stones surrounding finer soil in alpine tundra, formed by freezing and thawing of water in soil above permanently frozen ground.

G

garnet: an igneous or metamorphic mineral group of the general formula $A_3B_2(SiO_4)_3$, where A is Mg, Fe^{++}, Mn, or Ca, and B is Al, Fe^{+++}, Ti, or Cr; often dark red, brownish, or green; no *cleavage*.

geobotany: the study of plants as indicators of geological processes.

glacial erratic: a free-standing boulder transported by a glacier.

glacial moraine: a heterogeneous mixture of generally rounded rock fragments of various rock types and sizes ranging from clay to boulders, moved and deposited by a glacier.

glacial outwash: *stratified* sand and gravel deposited downstream from a glacier *terminus* by meltwater streams and glacier outburst floods.

gneiss: a *metamporphic* rock in which bands of light, non-platy, minerals, like *feldspar* and *quartz*, alternate with bands of dark, platy, or linear minerals, like *biotite* and *hornblende*.

grade: an equilibrium *long-profile* on a stream representing a balance between erosion and deposition; usually a smooth curve, steeper in the headwaters and gentler toward the mouth.

gradient profile: see *grade*.

Grand Hogback monocline: a major flexure in the Earth's *crust*, passing south-southeastward through Glenwood Springs and blending with the Schofield syncline southwest of the Maroon Bells, therefore coinciding, on its southern end, with the west edge of the Elk Mountain *gravity glide sheet*. Uplift of the land east of the *monocline* has continued intermittently since about 72 million years ago.

granite: an *intrusive*, coarse-grained *igneous* rock of light color. Its essential minerals are orthoclase *feldspar* and *quartz*. Granite is the principal rock of continents.

granodiorite: an *intrusive igneous* rock similar to *granite*. Its essential minerals are sodic plagioclase *feldspar*, orthoclase *feldspar* (less than in *quartz monzonite*), and *quartz*.

gravity gliding: *landsliding*, involving a very large slide block, or gravity glide sheet, which usually slides on a weak stratum such as soft *shale*.

graywacke: impure *quartz sandstone* and *siltstone* with abundant fragments of volcanic and *metamorphic* rocks, mainly deposited as submarine mudflows in an ocean trench associated with volcanic island arcs off a continental margin.

Great Basin: the *faulted* and subsided region from eastern Oregon to western Utah south to southeast California and southern Arizona; the former site of the *Western Cordillera*.

groundmass: see *matrix*.

ground moraine: *glacial moraine* deposited as a sheet on the ground beneath a glacier.

gypsum: hydrous calcium sulfate, $CaSO_4 \bullet 2H_2O$; colorless and transparent when pure; bladed crystals with a perfect basal *cleavage*, and a fibrous prismatic *cleavage*. Usually formed by evaporation of seawater in a shallow, *epicontinental sea* with restricted circulation.

H

halite: sodium chloride, NaCl; in colorless and transparent cubic crystals when pure, with perfect cubic *cleavage*. Formed with *gypsum*, but usually from more concentrated brines.

hanging valley: a valley that enters another valley at some height above its floor. Typical of glaciated valley systems.

horn: a mountain peak which has been steepened by the action of two or more glaciers in *cirques* on its flanks.

hornfels: a baked *shale* or other fine-grained *clastic* rock.

I

ice cap: a thick sheet of glacial ice that forms on a high plain surface.

igneous: refers to a rock that has at some time passed through a completely molten state.

induration: the process of becoming hard, as in the cementing of sediments into *sedimentary* rock.

intrusion: invasion of *country rock* by a body of *magma*; a body of *igneous* rock that has invaded the country rock.

J

joint: a break in the Earth's *crust* along which no movement has taken place.

K

kame terrace: a deposit of semi-*stratified* sand and gravel between the margin of a melting glacier and the adjacent bedrock of the valley wall.

kettle pond: a pond whose basin was formed by the melting of a large, detached block of glacial ice immersed in *glacial moraine*.

Kula plate: a *basaltic* ocean floor plate lying to the north of the junction between the *Pacific plate* and the *Farallon plate* at the *East Pacific Rise*. The Kula plate has been totally *subducted* beneath the *North American plate*.

L

lag concentrate: a deposit of larger stones left after water or wind has flushed away the finer material from the original deposit.

landslide: the slow to rapid downslope movement of earth material or rock.

Laramide orogeny: a mountain-building episode, most active in the Rocky Mountain region between 72 and 57 million years ago, apparently controlled by a *shearing stress* placed on the *North American plate* by a southward shift in *continental drift* direction between 81 and 53 million years ago.

lateral moraine: *glacial moraine* deposited at the margin of a flowing glacier.

levee: (properly, *natural levee*) a deposit of gravel, cobbles, and boulders on either side of a flood or rockslide channel, made during floods or rockslides due to lower flow velocities adjacent to the mainstream.

limestone: a rock type consisting mainly of *calcite* deposited as a chemical precipitate or as accumulated *calcareous* shells of dead marine organisms.

limonite: a brown, hydrous oxide of iron of variable composition.

lithification: the process of turning into rock. See *induration*.

lithologic: having to do with rocks.

long-profile: the shape of a valley along its long axis.

M

magma: molten rock.

mantle: that portion of the Earth's interior between the *crust* and the core, whose boundary lies at a depth of about 1800 miles. The mantle is solid, and may consist either of peridotite or of a dense phase of *basalt* called eclogite.

matrix: the finer-grained material of a rock having more than one *mode* of grain size.

meander: a looplike bend in a river channel.

medial moraine: *glacial moraine* deposited beneath the suture between two coalescent glaciers.

metamorphic: refers to rocks which have been altered by environmental conditions greatly different from those under which the rock was originally formed (the term usually excludes *weathering.*)

Mid-Atlantic Ridge: a *spreading rift* that runs down the centerline of the Atlantic Ocean floor. The *North American plate* is growing westward from the Ridge at the same rate at which the Eurasian plate is growing eastward from it.

migmatite: a variety of *gneiss* in which *magma* has been injected between the *foliation planes.*

mine dump: a pile of rejected rock below a mine entrance.

mode: a characteristic value; a unimodal gravel has rock particles all of a uniform size, a bimodal gravel has particles of two distinctly different sizes, a trimodal gravel has particles of three different sizes, and so on.

monocline: a steplike fold in otherwise essentially horizontal layered rocks.

mud flow: a flood in which the volume of mud and rock may equal or exceed the volume of water.

mudstone: an indurated mud; unlaminated *shale*; grain size up to 1/16mm.

muscovite: a mica, hydrous potassium aluminum silicate, $KAl_2(AlSi_3O_{10})(OH)_2$; clear, transparent, and with perfect basal *cleavage*, producing thin sheets.

N

Nevadan orogeny: a mountain-building episode that involved the western margin of North American between about 151 and 81 million years ago.

nivation: ground excavation beneath permanent snowbanks by the seasonal freezing and thawing of meltwater.

North American plate: a plate of *basalt* extending from the *MidAtlantic Ridge* westward to the west coast to North America and bearing the *granitic* North American continent on its upper, western surface.

O

oil shale: *shale* with a high content of organic hydrocarbons.

olivine: forsterite: magnesium silicate, Mg_2SiO_4; and fayalite: iron silicate, Fe_2SiO_4; usually pistachio green; no cleavage.

orogeny: mountain-building, involving the folding, *faulting*, and *intrusion* of *country rock*.

oxidation: the combining of other atoms with oxygen; an important agent in the weathering of minerals and rocks.

P

Pangaea: an agglomeration of all the major continental plates that began about 360 million years ago and persisted until its fragmentation, which began about 200 million years ago.

pegmatite: a very coarse-grained *igneous intrusive*, usually *granite*.

phenocryst: a large crystal in a *porphyry* surrounded by a finer *matrix*.

plate tectonics: the study of the origins, motions, and interactions of the *basaltic* plates that make up the Earth's *crust*.

playa lake: a shallow, intermittent lake in a desert basin.

polygonal ground: regular patterns formed in loose soil and rock above permanently frozen ground due to seasonal cycles of freezing and thawing of surface moisture. The effect is to segregate coarse material into a network of stone rings surrounding finer soil.

porphyry: an *igneous intrusive* rock composed of larger *phenocrysts* surrounded by a finer-grained *matrix*.

protalus rampart: a ridge formed at the base of a snowfield, usually in a glacial *cirque*, where *talus* has slid down the snow surface.

pyrite: iron disulfide, FeS_2; no cleavage, but usually occurs in brassy yellow, cubic crystals.

pyrolusite: manganese dioxide, MnO_2; no cleavage; usually in massive, dull black deposits, but often in delicate, branching, mosslike incrustations.

pyroxene: a mineral group of the general formula $ABSi_2O_6$, where A may be Mg, Fe^{++}, Ca or, Na, and B may be Mg, Fe^{++}, or Al; colorless to (usually) black; poor prismatic *cleavage* with cleavage angles of about 87 and 93 degrees.

Q

quartz: silicon dioxide, SiO_2; colorless and transparent when pure, with a greasy luster and an irregular fracture, but no *cleavage*.

quartz latite: the fine-grained equivalent of *granodiorite*.

quartz monzonite: a coarse-grained, light-colored *igneous* rock similar to *granite*. Essential minerals are sodic plagioclase *feldspar*, orthoclase *feldspar* (more than in *granodiorite*), and *quartz*.

quartzite: *silica*-cemented quartz sandstone; usually dense and white with a sugary appearance on fresh fracture.

R

recessional moraine: a ridge of *glacial moraine* left across a valley during a temporary halt in the upvalley retreat of a glacier *terminus*.

regional uplift: broad, general uplift of a very large region without appreciable folding or *faulting* of the *country rock*.

riegel: a rock bar or "stairtread" across the long axis of a glaciated valley.

right-lateral: refers to a displacement along a *fault* or *shear zone* in which the side across the fault from the observer has moved to the right. If that side had moved to the left, the displacement would have been left-lateral.

ripplemarks: small, rhythmic ridges and valleys on a *bedding plane*, caused by wind or water currents.

rock unit: = *formation*

rockfall: = *rockslide:* the rapid downslope movement of essentially dry rock debris.

Rocky Mountain erosion surface: an extensive *erosional* plain developed in the Rocky Mountain region following the *Laramide orogeny*, now largely destroyed by subsequent canyon cutting, mainly during the last 10 million years.

S

sandstone: *indurated* sand; grain size 1/16mm to 2mm.

schist: a *metamorphic* rock dominated by closely spaced *foliation planes*.

sedimentary: deposited by or from fluid media, including wind, water, and ice.

sericite: very fine-grained *muscovite*.

Sevier orogeny: a mountain-building episode involving mainly western Utah between about 140 and 70 million years ago.

shale: *mudstone* with a definite lamination; grain size less than 1/256mm.

shear zone: a zone in which rocks have been deformed by innumerable small *faults*, all of which slipped in the same direction.

shearing stress: a force that tends to move one part of a body in a direction parallel to its plane of contact with another part.

shield volcano: a low, flat volcanic cone formed by the eruption of fluid, *basaltic* lava.

silica: silicon dioxide, SiO_2, whether *crystalline* or amorphous.

siliceous: containing *silica*.

sill: a tabular body of *intrusive igneous* rock that lies parallel to *bedding* or *foliation planes* in the *country rock*.

siltstone: *indurated* silt; grain size 1/256mm to 1/16mm.

slate: a *metamorphosed shale* or *mudstone* with *slaty cleavage*.

slaty cleavage: *foliation* in a fine-grained *metamorphic* rock due to the parallel growth of platy minerals, like *sericite*. Such rocks split readily along this *cleavage*.

slickensides: smoothed, grooved, and polished rock surfaces on either side of a *fault* plane.

slipoff slope: the gently-sloping, convex land surface of the inside bank of a stream bend.

soil creep: the slow, downslope movement of water-saturated soil.

soil ripples: washboard-like ripples in soil on steep slopes.

spreading rift: a crack in the Earth's *crust* within which *basaltic magma* rises from the *mantle*, and solidifies on the walls of the crack as they move apart from each other. This is the mechanism by which the *crustal* plates grow. Most spreading rifts are located on ocean floors.

springbowl: a *cirque*-like depression on a hillside caused by the flushing away of soil and rock debris by spring action.

stock: a body of *intrusive igneous* rock of non-tabular form, and measuring 40 square miles or less in its largest horizontal extent.

strata: homogeneous layers in *sedimentary* or volcanic rock.

T

talus: loose, angular rock debris accumulated toward the base of a slope or cliff.

tarn: a lake filling a glacially scoured rock depression in the floor of a *cirque*.

tectonic: related to forms created by the deformation of the Earth's *crust*.

tensional stress: a force tending to pull things apart.

terminal moraine: *glacial moraine* deposited at the farthest downvalley extension of a glacier *terminus*.

terminus: the downvalley end of a glacier.

Transcontinental Arch: a persistently high, stable region of the North American continent from about 600 to 300 million years ago, extending from Arizona to Minnesota.

travertine: calcium carbonate, $CaCO_3$, deposited from fresh water.

V

valley glacier: a glacier confined to a valley in its lower course.

vein: a thin, tabular body of *intrusive* rock, generally composed of minerals that are highly soluble in superheated water.

volcanic ash: fragments of solidified *magma* less than 4mm in diameter that have been ejected into the atmosphere from a volcano.

volcanism: the formation of volcanoes.

W

wallrock: *country rock* adjacent to an *intrusion* or a *vein*.

weathering: the breakdown of minerals under chemical and mechanical processes at the Earth's surface, including *oxidation*, corrosion (mainly by carbonic acid in rainwater and around plant roots), frost wedging, temperature changes, and root wedging.

welded tuff: see *ash-flow tuff*.

Western Cordillera: a major mountain range developed from Alaska to southern Mexico during the *Nevadan* and *Sevier orogenies*.

Western Interior Seaway: see *Cretaceous seaway*.

Bibliography
(principal references starred)

Bryant, Bruce, 1969; Geologic map of the Maroon Bells quadrangle, Pitkin and Gunnison counties, Colo.; U.S. Geological Survey Geologic Quadrangle Map GQ-788.

* _____, 1970; Geologic map of the Hayden Peak quadrangle, Pitkin and Gunnison counties, Colo.; U.S. Geological Survey Geologic Quadrangle Map GQ-863.

* _____, 1971; Geologic map of the Aspen quadrangle, Pitkin County, Colo.; U.S. Geological Survey Geologic Quadrangle Map GQ-933.

_____, 1972; Geologic map of the Highland Peak quadrangle, Pitkin County, Colo.; U.S. Geological Survey Geologic Quadrangle Map GQ-932.

Clark, T.H., and Stearn, C.W., 1968; Geological evolution of North America, 2nd Ed.; Ronald Press Co., N.Y., 570 pp.

* *Curtis, Bruce F.,* Ed., 1975; Cenozoic history of the southern Rocky Mountains; Geological Society of America, Memoir #144.

Eardley, A.J., 1962; Structural geology of North America, 2nd Ed., Harper and Row, New York, 743 pp.

Fox, F.M. and Associates, 1974; Roaring Fork and Crystal Valleys; an environmental and engineering geology study; Colorado

Geological Survey, Environmental Geology Series #8, Denver.

Freeman, Val L., 1972; Geologic map of the Ruedi quadrangle, Pitkin and Eagle Counties, Colo.; U.S. Geological Survey Geologic Quadrangle Map GQ-967.

Gaskill, D.L., and Godwin, L.H., 1966; Geologic map of the Marble quadrangle, Gunnison and Pitkin counties, Colo.; U.S. Geological Survey Geologic Quadrangle Map GQ-512.

**Hintze, Lehi F.*, 1973; Geologic history of Utah; Brigham Young University Geology Studies, Vol. 20, Part 3, Studies for Students #8, 181 pp.

Leopold, E.B., and MacGinitie, H.D., 1972; Development and affinities of Tertiary floras in the Rocky Mountains, *in* Graham, A., Ed., Floristics and paleofloristics of Asia and eastern North America; Elsevier Publ. Co., Amsterdam; pp. 147-200.

* *Mallory, William W.*, Ed., 1972; Geologic Atlas of the Rocky Mountain region; Rocky Mountain Association of Geologists, Denver, 331 pp.

Mutschler, Felix E., 1970; Geologic map of the Snowmass Mountain quadrangle, Pitkin and Gunnison Counties, Colo.; U.S. Geological Survey, Geologic Quadrangle Map GQ-853.

Oetking, Philip, 1967; Geological highway map of the southern Rocky Mountain region; American Association of Petroleum Geologists, Tulsa.

O'Shea, Michael, 1975; The new Aspen area trail guide; O'Shea, Aspen, Colo.; 40 pp.

* *Petersen, M.S., Rigby, J.K., and Hintze, L.F.*, 1973; Historical geology of North America; Wm. C. Brown Co., Dubuque; 193 pp.

Seifert, C.K., and Siskin, L.A., 1973; Earth history and plate tectonics, an introduction to historical geology; Harper and Row; 504 pp.

Tidwell, William D., 1975; Common fossil plants of Western North America; Brigham Young University Press, Provo, Utah; 197 pp.

Tweto, Ogden, 1968; Geologic setting and interrelationships of mineral deposits in the mountain province of Colorado and south-central Wyoming; *in* Ridge, J.D., Ed., Ore deposits of the

United States, 1933-1967, Graton-Sales Volume; Amer. Inst. Min. Met. Petrol. Eng.; pp. 552-588.

* *Tweto, O., Moench, R.H., and Reed, J.C., Jr.*, 1976; Preliminary geologic map of the Leadville 1 degree × 2 degree quadrangle, northwestern Colorado; U.S. Geological Survey Miscellaneous Field Studies Map MF-760.

U.S. Forest Service, 1973; Forest visitors map, White River National Forest, Colorado.

* *Wise, J.P., and Heidrick, T.L.*, 1976; Preliminary report, Aspen district, Pitkin County, Colorado; unpublished report, Rosario Exploration Co., Tucson, Ariz., 45 pp.